D0553334

THE HUNGER

LINCOLN TOWNLEY

Cork City Libraries
WITHDRAWN
FROM STOCK

**SIMON &
SCHUSTER**

London · New York · Sydney · Toronto · New Delhi

A CBS COMPANY

First published in Great Britain by Simon & Schuster UK Ltd, 2014
A CBS COMPANY

Copyright © Lincoln Townley, 2014

This book is copyright under the Berne Convention.
No reproduction without permission.
All rights reserved.

The right of Lincoln Townley to be identified as the author of this work
has been asserted in accordance with sections 77 and 78 of
the Copyright, Designs and Patents Act, 1988.

1 3 5 7 9 10 8 6 4 2

Simon & Schuster UK Ltd
1st Floor
222 Gray's Inn Road
London WC1X 8HB

www.simonandschuster.co.uk

Simon & Schuster Australia, Sydney
Simon & Schuster India, New Delhi

A CIP catalogue record for this book
is available from the British Library.

ISBN (Paperback): 978-1-47113-541-5
ISBN (Ebook): 978-1-47113-542-2

Typeset in Aldine by M Rules
Printed and bound by CPI Group (UK) Ltd, Croydon, CR0 4YY

This book is dedicated to my wife Denise,
for helping me become the man I am today.

Contents

This is my story.

I have changed dates, times and occasionally places to protect those involved. I have also re-named some people and places and sometimes created composite characters from the people I knew. What I have not changed is what I did or the nature of my addiction.

Prologue

And a Man sat alone, drenched deep in sadness.

And all the animals drew near to him and said, 'We do not like to see you so sad. Ask us for whatever you wish and you shall have it.'

The Man said, 'I want to have good sight.'

The vulture replied, 'You shall have mine.'

The Man said, 'I want to be strong.'

The jaguar said, 'You shall be strong like me.'

Then the Man said, 'I long to know the secrets of the earth.'

The serpent replied, 'I will show them to you.'

And so it went with all the animals. And when the Man had all the gifts that they could give, he left.

Then the owl said to the other animals, 'Now the Man knows much, he'll be able to do many things. Suddenly I am afraid.'

The deer said, 'The Man has all that he needs. Now his sadness will stop.'

But the owl replied, 'No. I saw a hole in the Man, deep like a Hunger he will never fill. It is what makes him sad and what makes him want. He will go on taking and taking, until one day the World will say, "I am no more and I have nothing left to give."'

Old Storyteller from *Apocalypto*

The Hunger

August 2009. 7 a.m.

Addiction is ugly.

And relentless.

I am running. My heart is pounding. Thrashing at my ribcage. Wanting to burst through and splatter on the ground. I see blood everywhere. Guts and spleen. Keep running.

There must be people around. I am moving past them, through them. They are shadows. All I can feel is the rage of my heart and the thud of my feet on the pavement. I am smothering in my own breath. There is no way out. It has gone too far.

There are strangers in my bed. I do not know who they are or how they got there: a mass of banged-up oestrogen, propped up, surrounded by lube, cocaine and condoms, an altar to my solitude. I am sprinting and my head is exploding. I am floating. Dying. People look horrified and let me pass. They part as I drive through them. They can see I'm running. And I cannot be stopped.

1 a.m. Six hours earlier

Tina is lying face down on the bed, her arse spread, a line of coke stretching from her mid-back to her crack. I am snorting it when the intercom buzzes. I finish my line and the vodka on the bedside table, slip on a dressing gown and walk out to the hall. It's Rachel. She sent me a text earlier with a naked picture attached, asking if she could join us. I'm expecting three more Regulars and a Paid-For.

One by the one they arrive. They try to make small talk. I'm not interested. I ask if they want a drink. They all do. I send them into the bedroom and tell them to strip. I'm off my head, which means I've given myself permission to be more of a twat than usual. Katie is the last to arrive.

—You happy, Linc?

—All good. Go and join them and I'll be with you in a second.

I go to the bathroom and take a sachet of Kamagra. I take one on Tuesday and one on Thursday, so there's always some floating about in my system. The gel acts faster than the tablet and, when I come into the bedroom, my cock is rock solid. Four of the girls are on the bed while two, including Katie, are lying on the floor sharing a couple of lines with Tina. Katie is tall with long, willowy blonde hair. The first time I met her was in the bar at a Soho hotel. We went to the toilets and, before I could rip her dress to shreds, she laid out two lines on the seat and said:

—Coke before cock, Lincoln, always remember that.

The girls are all naked and they do not know there is a Man in the corner sitting on my best chair dressed in a long, black morning coat, starched white shirt with matching crimson cravat and handkerchief. He raises a glass of red wine and smiles at me. I smile back. The Man has been in my life, in one form or another, as long as I can remember. I used to think I was going crazy when other people didn't hear him or even see him. I thought they were winding me up, so I would point at him and shout:

—He's there! Look at him! He's real!

Then I realised they couldn't see him. He laughed at me:

—I am your dirty little secret, Lincoln, your dirtiest little secret!

I look across at him and he takes off his bowler hat, flicks his mop of ruffled black hair and lies on the floor next to the girls. He runs his finger along Tina's back before stretching his pointed tongue around Katie's neck. The girls shudder and look around. They sense the presence of the Man but they can't see him, so they carry on snorting. The Man angles his head towards me in a gesture of triumph as his face breaks into a rakish laugh. He says:

—Let's have some fun, Lincoln. I'm ravenous!

The Paid-For is staring at my cock. Her eyes are a little too wide and she's too clean, so I pick her first. I lay her on the floor and pound her for about an hour. She may be a hooker but she's never been fucked like this before. Her eyes are bulging and I worry in case they pop out of her head and hit me in the face.

When I'm finished with her she can't move. She is delirious. I line up the other girls, arses out, and fuck them one at a time. Tina is in hysterics and can't stop laughing. I tell her to shut up because she's putting me off. She winks at me and begins ramming a butt plug in Sandra, who is trying to keep her head steady above a line of coke. We're at it for about five hours. I come twice then I fall asleep. An hour later I wake up and my bedroom is in chaos. I am shaking and my throat is dry. I look around. The Man is nowhere to be seen. I get dressed and go out for an eight-mile run through the city.

10 p.m. Three hours earlier

I'm at The Office in Soho. It's not an office like the ones where people waste their lives getting things done. It's actually a bar where I work at creating Chaos. The boys are all upstairs getting hammered, as the smell of food wafts from the kitchen into the disabled toilet where I'm working. Before I took her to the toilet, the girl, whose name I can't remember, said:

—My boyfriend is meeting me here.

—He's not here now, is he?

—Well . . .

I place my hand on her wrist and she looks deep into my coked-out eyes.

—I really want to fuck you.

And now I'm hammering her so hard in the toilet that the pan cracks. I think I must remember to tell Mario, the manager. It's the decent thing to do. Then I focus on the pounding and forget what it was I had to remember. My memory isn't jogged even when a big chunk of china breaks off and hits the floor.

When we walk back upstairs into the restaurant the boys are looking worried. I notice a tall guy towering above them. As soon as he sees me and the girl he walks over to us. He is not happy.

—Where have you been?

The girl is silent. He tries to take a swipe at her. I block his arm. She is crying and shaking, her dress torn at the seam. I may be a twat but I'm a considerate one and I don't like bullies.

—Try that again and I'll deck you.

He looks at me and takes another swipe. This time at me. I warned him. I hit him with two punches – one to the solar plexus and another to the side of the neck. He drops unconscious to the floor. The girl screams.

—You've killed him! You've killed him!

I think perhaps I have. Mario rushes towards me.

—Fucking hell, Lincoln. Take it easy. My God, I think you've killed him.

I wonder if Mario is a mind reader, then I look at the lifeless body on the floor and I realise he's stating the fucking obvious.

Maynard and Terry get up off the table and throw two glasses of wine over the man's face.

—That was a fucking waste!

—Sorry, Linc, we're only trying to help.

I lean over him and press my ear to his chest. He's still breathing. I look at the girl and think she looks so sexy in that torn dress. I want to fuck her again. NOW. The man rolls his head to one side and groans. I want to knock him out again. I NEED him unconscious. Just another twenty minutes. That's all I crave. Mario props him up and soon he is standing. He sees me and tries to lift his arm but it falls limp against the bar. I walk up to him.

—Don't even think about it, and if you lay one finger on your girl, I'll fucking kill you.

He doesn't respond. I grab him by the collar. No one tries to stop me.

—Do you hear me?

He nods.

—I didn't fucking hear you.

—Yes ... yes ...

I walk over to the girl and give her my card. Lincoln Townley, Sales and Marketing Director, The Club.

—If he gives you any trouble call me and I'll deal with him.

She has mascara all over her face.

—Thanks.

Outside on the street, the Man with the crimson cravat, whose name is Esurio, is leaning against a wall, smoking a cigar.

—That was splendid, Lincoln, splendid. Where shall we go next?

—Fuck off!

—Now that is an absurd idea. I couldn't possibly fuck off when we're having such fun!

3 p.m. Seven hours earlier

My favourite hour of the day. The Gym, Soho.

Most people want to get fit. Build some muscle. I don't. I just want to go fucking mental. I begin with twenty minutes on the treadmill. Sprinting. Then a hundred press-ups on my knuckles in under two minutes. There's a reason I do press-ups on my knuckles. I severed the tendon in my right wrist bench-pressing 120kg ten years ago. It hurt. Pain like I've never experienced before or since. The surgeon said the best he could do was to fuse it together again but it would be rigid like a pole. I said no. Then the pain got even worse and I went to him and asked:

—Can you please cut my hand off?

He said no. But he did the operation and, after a couple of years, it was more or less normal. I can't bend it fully or put too much pressure on it. Other than that, it's fine. One strange thing: I still wank and wipe my arse with my left hand. Which goes to prove that habits can be changed when the pain gets too intense. That thought comes to my mind as I bench press 100kg. I say to myself:

—That's a good observation, Lincoln.

Then I forget it and carry on with the circuit: 200 curls, 150 sit-ups, 50kg lat-pulls and on into exhaustion. The last lift: 100kg bench-press. My teeth clench and I scream:

—Push! Push, you fucker! Push!

My eyes get caught in the lights of the gym and I can hear the same words:

—Push! Push! Push!

It's a woman's voice. I blink hard and turn my eyes away from the light. I am nineteen and holding my girlfriend's hand. The midwife continues with her mantra:

—Push! Push! Push!

First the head. Then the screaming, bloodied body, and a few minutes later I am holding my son, Lewis, in my arms. I think:

- I know I am happy to die for my son
- I know I love my son

- I know I do not love my girlfriend
- I know I will marry my girlfriend
- I know my marriage will end

I can't remember the day I got I married. I can remember the day it ended. Lewis was eighteen months old and my life, free and full of possibility, felt like a Dark Desert. This is what I learned in the Desert:

- I can lose my wife and smile
- I cannot lose my son and live
- I understand true love for the first time

When I leave The Gym, I walk over to The Club and down a bottle of Rioja and I'm just starting on the shots when Maynard, Terry, Simon and Steve join me.

11 a.m. Four hours earlier

The Boss watches me walk into The Club. I think he hasn't seen me grip the door handle to stop me falling to the ground. There are only half a dozen offices in the basement of The Club and they are built from floor-to-ceiling glass panels – of course, he hasn't seen me! I smile at him as I walk into my office. He smiles back. He's thinking:

—You're fucked, Lincoln.

I'm thinking:

—You're fucked, Lincoln.

George, Jack and Mark, his business partners and Joy, his secretary, are all there. They're all in their sixties and seventies and have been together for decades. I've been here three months and it's fair to say opinion about me is divided:

George thinks I am a cunt and doesn't want me anywhere near the clubs.

Jack thinks I am a cunt and believes I am the best sales director he's ever worked with.

Mark thinks I am a cunt and, like any good accountant, doesn't give a fuck as long as I keep bringing the punters in.

Joy is too nice to think anyone is a cunt.

And The Boss thinks I am a *flash* cunt and I think that is the biggest compliment anyone has ever paid me.

Although the offices are just about big enough to swing a cat in, The Boss has invented his own, unique internal communication system. It's a fucking bell that sits on his desk, one of those old-fashioned brass ones where you hit a little knob on the top. Each of us has a number of rings allocated to our name. I am five rings and, as soon I sit down, the bell rings five times. I squeeze my eyes tight shut as my head feels like the biggest, boomiest bell chamber in the world. I get up and walk ten feet to his office.

—How many times, Lincoln?

He is staring at me.

I hate that stare.

If I had to put a name to it I would call it *paternal* and that's what I hate. If he was a tosser, a typical Soho club owner, all ego and no heart, I wouldn't give a shit. But he's neither. The Boss is a one-off and I love him.

—What?

—Don't give me 'what'. Sit down.

I sit down. My chair is lower than his.

—You can't fool me, Lincoln. I've seen it all. You stumble into my office off your head. You can barely stand. How many times have I told you, you're going to kill yourself? Worse than that, you're going to kill off my punters.

—Give me a break, Boss. You know I can fill the clubs better than anyone.

—I'm always giving you breaks. I give you breaks when you shag yourself to exhaustion. I give you breaks when you don't know what day it is. I give you breaks when George tells me to kick you out. How many more breaks do you want?

He's right except for one little word. I don't 'want' breaks. I 'need' them. Thousands of them. Now and tomorrow and the day after and every day after that. Without them I'm in the shit, and I know the more air I pump into my ego, the higher it flies, the more likely I am to fall into some dirty, narrow little gutter where I will disappear without trace. Some people have even been kind enough to point this out to me. One of them was Frank. He was my boss before I worked at The Club and he ran one of the biggest transport companies in the country. I was the youngest and best Sales Director he ever employed. I wasn't drinking too much then. No drugs at all. I whored a bit but other than that I was in a stable relationship. I bought my first Ferrari, a 355 Berlinetta, when I was twenty-five, and my Mum still has a photograph of me holding a monthly pay cheque for sixteen grand. She told me to use my money wisely. She might as well have told a Banker to stop investing in strippers. When the money was gone I made a list of *Wise Things I Did With My Money Before I Blew It.* It was a short list. This was it:

• Fun days out with my son, Lewis.

I had him every weekend. I took him to fairs, amusement arcades, played conkers and football with him, cooked him roast dinners, sent paper planes into orbit and I paid his maintenance without ever missing a month. Not much wisdom, I agree, but enough to keep me sane. When I picked him up in my Ferrari he said:

—Daddy, go fast! Go fast!

When I didn't go fast, he said:

—Why slow?

The reason was simple. I was in a convoy with my salesmen on a motorway when they began racing each other. Jim, one of my sales managers, was in the lead when he flipped over the central reservation and flew into the grill of a fucking monster truck. I saw the windows of his car splash with blood as his body burst open like a tomato. I never drove my Ferrari or any other car over seventy. So I said:

—Slow is better, Lewis.

He reminded me of that a few weeks ago when he found me slumped over a stripper, coke still stuck between my teeth. I said:

—I know, son, I just can't find the brakes anymore.

When I was Sales Director in the transport business, I managed over two hundred salesmen. I was a Great Motivator. There were prizes and promises and praise but that was never enough. That gets you liked. What gets you respected, what drives a hairy-arsed salesman to bring in a deal like his life depends on it, is when he thinks his life really does depend on it. I call it the *Power of Fear* and no one used it better than me. Men in their forties and fifties who'd been selling since they were in nappies would be terrified to come in to work without a deal to their name. Fear made them my Bitches and

Bitches sell best because the price of an unsold lead is more than they can afford to pay.

When one of the salesmen left the company and decided to take the company car with him, I took it personally. He was in the car when I found him. He tried to drive away so I jumped on the bonnet and cracked the glass with my fist. He pulled over and I dragged him out. He went on his knees and said:

—Sorry, Lincoln. Please don't hurt me.

I took the keys and left him, crying like a baby, on the side of the road.

When I got back, Frank said:

—There's no one I have ever met with as little middle ground as you, Lincoln. You'll end up in the gutter or the stars. I just don't know which.

The Boss, says:

—Do you hear me, Lincoln?

He points to the photographs on the walls. The biggest stars in the world look down on me. Mick Jagger, Paul McCartney, John Lennon, Jack Nicholson, Bruce Willis, Elton John, Princess Diana. A pantheon of celebrity with him at the centre of it. He carries on:

—You can do what I did but not if you don't clean yourself up. Now get out and sort yourself out.

When I'm back in my office, George comes in. He is doing his best to appear calm. He says:

—I don't know how you hold on to your job. He's never been like this with anyone in fifty years.

—Because I'm good, George.

—No one is *that* good.

I smile. He is polite because he has to be. I know he wants

to smack me in the mouth and I know I deserve it. I am good. I am probably *that* good. But work is just the skin of my life, taking in enough money to feed the Hunger and that Hunger is the reason I stand on the face of the earth. Nothing else matters.

The Boss said once:

—I see a lot of me in you.

And that's how I survive. I am his mongrel child, a bastard mix of charisma and chaos, who looks as if I might just about make it until I fuck up and everything is wasted.

Esurio walks in and rests his right hand on the ornate silver skull that sits on top of his cane.

—We're still employed then, and the day is young.

—Give me an hour and I'll be with you.

—Make it sooner, Lincoln. You know how impatient I get.

9 a.m. Two hours earlier

I am back at the flat, my body glistening with sweat.

The girls are still in my bedroom so I shower and leave. My hands are shaking and my head is full of shit. I try to look straight and fix on a point at the far end of Old Compton Street. I can't even hold my gaze. I need a drink. Some coke. A drink. A line. Anything to take this feeling away. I want to be sick. I have a meeting at The Club. I can't let them see me fucked. I catch my reflection in a window. I think I look better than I feel. Grey suit. Open-neck shirt. White handkerchief. All I need is a drink, a line, to make the suit sparkle. I can see Esurio standing outside Cafe Boheme. He is holding the door open for me. I walk across the road.

—Thanks, man.

—My pleasure.

I go downstairs into the toilet and pull a wrap out of the inside pocket of my suit. By the time I'm walking up the stairs I feel more like myself. I'm sure the day will be good. Esurio is still standing outside by the door. When he sees me coming he pushes it open.

—Better?

—Yes, thanks.

I walk across the road to an off-licence. Coke is good. Two shots of vodka will make it immense. As I leave the shop and make my way to The Club, I raise a bottle to Esurio. He raises his hat.

—Here's to a beautiful day!

I smile at him. I love him. I hate him. He is a pest. A parasite. He never leaves me alone. I try to remember how we first met. I can't. It feels like he's always been with me. When I was a kid he was more ghostly than he is now. It was like I could see through him. There was the time when I was fourteen. A year after my Dad died. I was being bullied at school by a kid called Mitch Walters. He was a tall kid, a boxer. No one messed with him. Before he died, Dad said:

—No one ever pushes us around, Lincoln. No one.

My Granddad Bob said:

—We're fighters. Hit him back. Just once. So he knows he can't mess with you. Then leave him alone. He won't touch you again.

The next day I was at school. Mitch Walters was drinking a cup of hot chocolate. I snatched the cup out of his hand, threw the liquid in his face and punched him once.

—Just once, Lincoln.

Then, faint against the red brick of the school wall, I saw Esurio. Half his face was missing and so was most of the left side of his body, and it was like I could see through the rest of him. His voice was a waspish whisper, not as strong as it is now:

—Hit him again and again and again. Feed me, Lincoln, feed me.

I saw fear in the kid's eyes. I was a rabid dog. In seconds his head was like a ball on a spring. It spun in all directions as one punch then another clattered against his head. I knew I was going to kill him. I could not stop. I wanted to splatter his blood on the schoolyard. Rip out his guts and impale them on the fence. Then he stopped moving. Esurio waved his hands extravagantly:

—Wonderful! Wonderful! Carry on like this and we'll be partners for life!

Mitch survived. He wore a bandage around his head for weeks. His left ear was shattered and he will never hear properly again. Whenever he saw me he lowered his head and hunched his shoulders. His smile was the grimace of the defeated. Everyone thought I was insane. They were right. No one bothered me ever again.

A year before I beat the fuck out of Mitch Walters, my Dad died and Esurio was with me there too. I was running through a caravan park where we were staying when Dad dropped dead of a heart attack. I rushed into our caravan to get Mum, but she had already seen him collapse through the window. When I came back out again a man was trying to resuscitate my Dad. When I got to my father I could hear Esurio:

—We'll be fine from now on, Lincoln, fine. Just the two of us.

I turned to see where the voice was coming from but all I could see was a faint outline of a black morning coat a few yards away, with the white of the caravans and the blue of the sky pushing through it to create a messy patchwork of colour.

The first time I remember him fully formed like other people was when I was sixteen. I was shagging one of my Mum's best friends. She was fifty-two. I didn't have a place to live, so we fucked either in her house or in the back of a knackered Ford Fiesta I lived in for three months. One night, there he was, sitting on the bonnet of the car as I was pounding away, a ridiculous purple umbrella protecting him from the rain. He wiped the rain off the windscreen to get a better view.

—That's very impressive indeed. Quite the little pounder, aren't we? I predict great things for you, Lincoln.

And, to get great things, I needed great stages but selling vans can never be enough for a man with an appetite for Greatness. In 2009 I left the transport industry and took off to Ibiza to get my head together. I knew the island well. When Lewis was twelve, my ex-wife took him to Spain to live. That was the first time I thought I would lose him. The second was when he turned fifteen and I thought:

—I've lived long enough to see him past the age I was when my Dad died. What use am I to him now?

And one morning when I was having a coffee in Portals, looking out at the yachts in the harbour, this thought came back to me. It was one of those days that are so beautiful it hurts. The kind that magnifies the feeling of being a useless cunt. I had been sitting there maybe an hour when The Boss came in. He lives in Ibiza, and I knew him well because I had brought hundreds of van salesmen into his clubs. We had always got on and, before he left, he placed his business card on the table and said:

—Come and help me promote the clubs.

Even driftwood is going somewhere and, two months later, I arrived in Soho, the new Sales and Marketing Director of The Club. On the flight from Ibiza, Esurio sat next to me. He was no longer an uncertain presence in my life, and on that flight he was radiant. He stroked the carnation in his lapel:

—I got it especially for the flight. Rather beautiful, don't you think?

—Yeah, it's OK.

—Oh come on, don't be a party pooper! We're going to have the time of our lives. Sex, strippers, Soho. A stage fit for us to stand on.

Esurio has always been a clever cunt. Smarter than me. More agile. He often says:

—You're different from the rest, Lincoln. More extreme and more malleable. Two of the qualities I most appreciate in a man.

Despite the good times and the praise, I often wish we had never met. These are the things I hate most about him:

- He is so fucking arrogant
- He thinks he knows me better than I do
- He tells me he always knows what's good for me
- He thinks he's always right
- He gets inside my head and fucks with my mind
- He takes me for granted
- He speaks with a posh accent and says his father was a baronet

- He repeats himself in the same sentence like when he says: Feed me, Lincoln, feed me
- He is so fucking demanding and nothing I do ever satisfies him
- He knows I am in awe of him
- I hate him because he is stronger than me and he has a temper like a fucking tornado. One night, I didn't want to go out with him. I was sitting in the lounge watching Carol Vorderman on daytime TV. I wanted a day without a drink. Just a fucking day. He hated it. Started shouting at me. I said:

—Fuck off and leave me alone.

—Well, if that's what you want, Lincoln, I will fuck off. I'll go off into the hall and all the while you're watching TV I'll be lifting those weights of yours and doing press-ups, getting even stronger, Lincoln, even stronger, and I'll be so strong I'll be able to lift you like a feather and carry you wherever I want.

Two hours later I was in the Townhouse on Dean Street getting hammered.

- I hate his name. Esurio. So fucking pompous. I never understood why someone who sounds so English should have a Spanish name. I asked him:

—Are you Spanish?

—Latin, Lincoln, Latin.

—That's what I mean, Spanish.

—No, not that Latin. I'm referring to the ancient Italic language. The language of gods and emperors.

—What the fuck are you talking about?

—Esurio, Lincoln, is a Latin word.

—Oh yeah, what's it mean, then?

He stopped for a moment, raised his glass and smiled:

—Hunger, Lincoln, it means hunger.

Wraps

September 2009

—This is the place for us, Lincoln. Look at this . . . and this!

Esurio is beside himself with excitement. Soho has one language and that is the language of desire. It promises and teases. This is the land of make-believe where whatever you want you can have; where all you have to do is reach out and take it. Most people float in and out of Soho. They come looking for a fantasy and whether they find it or not, they leave. There are others who *think* they can float in and out but the breeze that blows them in is too weak to carry them out. These are the real victims of Soho. They come in search of freedom and find themselves trapped in a square mile of Chaos. I divide them into two groups:

Lost Men

These are middle-aged men. Some as young as thirty, most over fifty. Perhaps they have skirted around the edges of the film or television industry and now that they have surrendered their youth, their homes and their ambition to their ex-wives, they come looking to reverse time. They are happily looking forward to puberty and the joys of having a cock hard enough to use.

Hopeful Girls

Most of these are young models balancing their Louis Vuitton handbags on wobbly stilettos, who came to chase dreams and found a nightmare of coke and cock from which they will never escape. Others come from as far as São Paulo or St Petersburg to work in 'a great English city' and support their families back home. They, too, find a nightmare of coke and cock.

Soho connects these Lost Men and Hopeful Girls. It bundles them together in a stuffy little bag, and every day that passes the string around the top of the bag pulls a little tighter until the light and the air have gone and all that's left is the slow suffocation of hope.

Then there are those who come to Soho and hurl themselves at its core, daring it to do its worst and, when it does, they ask for more. Esurio says:

—That's you, Lincoln!

As usual he's right. I would like to say the descent into madness was gradual. First a drink, then a fuck, then another drink, then another fuck, then a line, then another line, then another, and on into Chaos. Sadly, that is not the case. Esurio makes sure the descent is fast and total, with not a cell in my nervous system left untouched within hours of arriving in Soho.

Esurio insists I live in a shared flat on Old Compton Street and, to be fair to him, it does make practical sense.

—You can walk to work from here and you won't have to worry about getting home at night. It's absolutely perfect!

But then I'm just kidding myself. When I'm surrounded by coke and cunt, 'practical sense' is just a disguise, a way of getting my excuses in early and, when I tell them to my Mum, they sound pretty convincing:

—Well, I need to be close to the clubs; or

—The Boss really wants me to be in the heart of Soho; or (and this is the best and curiously honest excuse):

—I want to show I'm a keen worker

And really, I am the keenest fucking worker in Soho. Here's what I have to do:

1. My number one priority is to fill the clubs with the right kind of punter.
2. Once I've got enough of the right kind of punter into the clubs I have to get them in *more than once*. Preferably every fucking week.
3. Then I have to help the girls be as good at selling as I am. This means I teach them to get the men into the private booths at three hundred quid an hour plus champagne at anything from five hundred to five grand a bottle. On the surface that seems quite easy. A man can have all the money in the world but when the girls start working him he's just a hapless fucking ape, dragging his knuckles on the ground, following the scent of pussy until he collapses from exhaustion. The one problem I have is that three things cloud my judgement, and if you could print out the contents of my brain at any frozen moment in time it would look like this: Drink. Coke. Cunt.

Drink. Coke. Cunt. Drink. Coke. Cunt. Drink.
Coke. Cunt. Drink. Coke. Cunt. Drink. Coke.
Cunt. Drink. Coke. Cunt. Drink. Coke. Cunt.
Drink. Coke. Cunt. Drink. Coke. Cunt. Drink.
Coke. Cunt. Drink. Coke. Cunt.

And putting me in charge of three hundred strippers is like putting the Taliban in charge of Homeland Security. Tonight I'm running a party for the City boys. Before they fucked the world economy, the Bankers had an easier time of it. Now they've been told they have to be a bit more careful. Rik is a hedge fund manager. He's younger than me, maybe thirty-five and almost as hammered as I am. He drives an Aston and a Bentley, fully loaded with an expense account big enough to fill the boot with cocaine. When he walks into The Club, he is with his accountant, Steve. Rik says:

—Can't even be let out on my own anymore, can I, Steve? The Chairman says we have to be responsible now. He was on the news the other day coming out with all this crap about how we have to sign up to a code of morals or fuck off. Apparently we're not interested in fast, easy money anymore. He says the rules have changed. We've got to have more respect. Think for the long term. In a way I agree with him. Which is why I've brought Steve with me. He will monitor carefully the money I spend on the girls and champagne and he will confirm that I am responsible for a morale-building evening of 'Corporate Entertainment'. Isn't that right, Steve?

Steve nods and finishes his Jack Daniel's. Rik touches my shoulder. I hate being touched by people I don't love. I don't love Rik. He must sense it and pulls back. Then he says:

—All there is, Linc, is naked self-interest. We are the species of *Me*. There are no morals. Not anymore. There never were any. It was always a game for losers. We'll bust the planet a thousand times, and as long as it's got enough left in the tank to get itself together again, we'll bust it again. And while all this shit is happening and little people are running for cover, we'll sound as if we care and carry on until there's nothing left to bust. Now, take me to the pussy.

Rik closes his eyes, sticks his arms out front and lets Steve guide him to a table near the stage. There are young girls everywhere, most in lingerie; some already have their tits out. I call them Wraps because for me young girls come bundled with alcohol and cocaine. They're all in the same box, impossible to separate one from another. I need a drink. I need some gear. I need a fuck. Put those sentences in any order you want and the meaning is always the same. You take the drugs away and the Wraps lose their purpose. You take the Wraps away and the drink is liquid loneliness.

My life is Chaos. I pound Wraps for fame and pleasure. If I have to choose the greater of the two, I always choose fame. In my head I have a map of *How It All Works*. One day I write it down.

How It All Works

The women I bang are split into five groups:

Regulars. This is the largest and most rewarding group of Wraps. To count as a Regular, I have to fuck a particular Wrap at least four times a month for three consecutive months.

Occasionals. These are Wraps I sleep with every month but no more than twice a month for two consecutive months.

One-Offs. Wraps I pull or who pull me and I never see again. There are many reasons I never see them again. Some are just passing through but mostly they prefer a man who will tuck them in bed and read them a story after it's over. Generally, I ask them to leave and, if they are unable to understand my request, I walk out, leaving them plenty of time to think about what it might mean.

Paid-Fors. I like this group because I can order what I want in advance and know with absolute certainty I will get it delivered. There are variations but A-levels and a willingness to be tied up are a staple of every order I make.

Grannies. This is the only non-Wrap category, since access to this group is only open to women between the ages of fifty and eighty. Technically, they can be older than eighty and still qualify but disability and dementia mean there is little point in leaving the upper age limit too open.

Statistics are an important part of *How It All Works*. Sometimes the hyperactive state of my nervous system leads to errors in record-keeping, but the distribution of activity between the five groups has been shown to break down as follows:

Regulars:	35%
Occasionals:	25%
One-Offs:	20%
Paid-Fors:	10%
Grannies:	10%

Other statistics that matter are the number of Wraps I bang in a month and their names, so I keep a list of both in my drawer to make sure everything is heading in the right direction. When I don't know or can't remember their names (which happens often) I write something like *Dark-Haired*

Girl, Hairless Hungarian or *Sparkly Stilettos*. I check these statistics at least twice a week.

Two of the most important aspects of *How It All Works* are
sales and marketing: how I get the Wraps in the first place, and
how I let the world know about my achievements. Sales and
marketing are all a bit knotted together and truth is in short
supply, but here's what I believe: on average I receive maybe
a dozen or so texts a day from Regulars and Occasionals wanting to know if I'm about and up for it. They also act as unpaid
sales agents and, quite often, a One-Off will text me with a
picture and write something like: *Joanna told me you're worth
trying out and I'd like to have a go. See you at the Townhouse at 11?
X.* I like these texts because it makes me feel I'm doing something useful with my life and making a difference in the
world.

Of course, I'm also a very proactive salesman, if a little pre-
dictable, since my pitches are usually a variation on: *I really
want to fuck you.* It might lack a degree of sophistication but it
works because I know my market and, contrary to some mali-
cious myths put forward by descendants of the Suffragettes,
women like being fucked. Really fucked. And when they get
it they want it again and again and nothing less will do until
they decide to get married and have kids. That's when they are
careful to choose a man who will look after them and not
notice when they disappear 'on business' for a night or two.

There is also the PR side of *How It All Works*. This is how
myths are created and I'm an accomplished myth-maker. It
usually happens in The Office but it can happen anywhere in
Soho. The technique is simple: I receive a text or an email or
I have a photograph of a recently banged Wrap and I show it
to anyone who wants to look at it, because I know that doing

it is of no value unless I am *seen* to be doing it. I am sure it pisses blokes off but what point is there in all the pounding if I'm doing something that any bloke could do? I particularly like the write-ups I get:

That's amazing!

How do you do it?

Not another one . . .

I also believe this creates more One-Offs, who may eventually graduate to become Regulars: Wraps fuck where other Wraps fuck, and this fact is the engine behind *How It All Works*. Wraps also like to fuck men who might dump them. An example: I was banging a stunning model called Lucy. I banged her for the last time in the Townhouse toilets. She said something I didn't like, so I left her sitting at the table waiting for her next cocktail. That earned me One-Offs from two Wraps who were sitting at the bar and saw what I did.

Women say they want men with morals. What they really want are men with status. The more Wraps a man dumps, the more status he gets and, the more status he gets, the more Wraps want him. I call it the *Wheel That Makes the World Go Round*.

There is, of course, the problem of boredom. A cunt is a cunt and the thousandth is no different from the first. This is where a good imagination helps. The Mind is its own place and can make a Whore of a Virgin, a Virgin of a Whore. I can shag anything because my Mind makes Wraps into whatever I want them to be. It keeps my cock going when my soul is dying. I said to Maynard once:

—Sometimes I feel as if I'm really shagging myself.

One final thing I notice is that Wraps like strong men, men

who will protect them, and I always look after my Wraps. I may fuck and leave them but if any bloke hassles them, I break his fucking legs. Here's the proof: I was with an Occasional and a One-Off in the Sanderson Hotel when a guy smacked one of them so hard on her arse she yelped. I broke a snooker cue on his back and knocked him unconscious with a bar stool. They both became Regulars.

More proof: I was walking past the entrance to the London Palladium when I saw a man threatening a Wrap I assumed was his girlfriend. I grabbed him by his shirt, lifted him up against the wall and said:

—If you want to act like a cunt, do it with me.

By the time I let him down, he decided he no longer wanted to act like a cunt and I banged his girlfriend in the toilets at Liberty's.

Selling the idea of getting your cock sucked is no different from selling vans. If you can do one, you can do the other. And I am the best at both. Here's an example: Terry was standing at the bar in The Office next to two Wraps. He said, 'Do you want a drink, girls?' They said, 'No.' I pushed past him, looked into their souls with my craziest coke-eyes and said: 'Vodka or champagne?' They said: 'Champagne.' I banged them both in the toilets after the second glass. Wraps, like any good customers, like to be told what to do. It makes them feel their babies will one day be in safe hands.

That's it. No secrets. *How It All Works* is how it has always worked: Wraps exchanging pussy for pleasure and protection.

3 p.m.

My day so far: two bottles of Rioja, three chocolate martinis, four bottles of Stella, a chilled bottle of Beaujolais, nine vodka tonics, a gram of coke, three hundred press-ups, a circuit at the gym, a seven-mile run and a sachet of Kamagra.

This is how my night goes:

9 p.m.

I'm not due at The Club for another hour, so I'm making great use of my time tying Suzie to my bed with her stockings. I've been pounding her for the last hour and she's been begging me to tie her up. I am, like all honest people, politically incorrect to my core. It's in a woman's nature to want to *submit* to a man, to crave a power greater than she feels herself to be, and there isn't a man on the face of the earth who doesn't want to feel a sexy bird swinging on the end of his cock or gasping at the size of his bank balance, screaming, 'Yes, Boss, anything you want, Boss.' Any bird who stays faithful to a weak man 'for the kids' then 'for the grandkids' then 'because it's the kind of woman I have become', will never find out how good it is to be well and truly fucked. She will, like all women, spend her nights dreaming about a Big Bang as she waits patiently for a bitter menopause.

Suzie is nineteen, five feet nothing, a mass of blonde hair, and begging for a butt plug.

—Tie me! Fuck me!

I've got her all trussed up when my phone rings. It's Rik. I can't remember what happened next.

9:45 p.m.

I must have left the flat because some Wrap whose name I don't know and who I've never met before is sucking my cock in the toilets at Little Italy. My phone rings again. *Unknown.* I fucking hate *Unknown.* If I know who it is I can choose to ignore it. *Unknown* is too open with possibility and I'm terrified of missing out.

—Yes.

—Is that Mr Townley?

'Mr' always means trouble. I pull my cock out of her mouth and send her out of the toilet.

—Who wants to fucking know?

—I'm a Police Officer and I am in your flat on Old Compton Street after a member of the public reported an incident.

In the future, a cell at the Police Station where this officer works will be like a second home to me and Esurio will say:

—Exposed brickwork. Off-white paintwork. Stone floor. Wrought-iron bed. Think of it like a loft conversion in Shoreditch. A bit smaller, I agree, and with a rather austere front door, but let's not worry about trifles!

But now it's just a place that might stand between me and my pleasure.

The Officer says:

—I understand you left a young girl tied up in your flat in Old Compton Street. Is that correct?

I hesitate. I need a drink. I need more coke. Then I say in an outburst of reckless honesty:

—Fuck! I forgot about Suzie!

—Forgot, Mr Townley? I think that's hardly credible.

Common sense would say that the officer is correct. It is highly unlikely that a man would forget he has a girl tied to his bed. Then, most things about my life are unlikely, including my shocking and deteriorating memory. In a brief, sober moment some days later, with the help of a police caution, I piece together what happened:

My phone rings.

It's Rik.

I don't answer it.

I forget the call.

Then I remember the call.

And the Bankers' Party.

I remember answering the call.

Which technically I didn't.

I stuffed the phone in Suzie's pussy when it rang.

She squeezed and answered it.

I think I've spoken to Rik.

Rik thinks I've dropped the phone in water and ends the call.

Rik says: Stupid cunt!

I think: I must go the Bankers' Party

I feel hungry.

I say: I must go to the kitchen.

I forget why I'm in the kitchen.

I remember I must go to The Club.

I get as far as Little Italy.

I forget why I'm there.

I remember Suzie.

I think: She's a great Wrap. Wouldn't mind seeing her again.

Suzie wonders where I am.

I wonder what Suzie is doing right now.

I see a Wrap.

I tell the Wrap: I want you to suck my cock.

She says: OK.

Suzie shouts: Help me! Help me!

My bedroom window is open.

A nice man hears her.

The nice man has two things you never see in Soho: a sober mind and a conscience.

I'm getting a shit blow-job in the toilets.

The nice man calls the police.

The police arrive.

They bash the wrong door down.

Then they bash the right door down and find Suzie.

The officer says: Are you all right?

Suzie says: Lincoln forgot about me. He gets forgetful sometimes. He's older than me.

I snort a line off the Wrap's head.

My phone rings.

I see good, inaccessible coke in the Wrap's hair.

I get angry.

It's the officer telling me he's found Suzie.

The next day I pay £125 for a new door. That pisses me off. I have a drink. Then a line. Then I feel pretty good about it all.

The new door is knotty pine.

I like knotty pine.

Esurio has been reading Tony Robbins. He thinks it's good for me to know these things. He says:

—It's not what you do, Lincoln. It's what you *learn* from it.

—Oh, fuck off. What can I learn from all this shit?

—How to do it better next time, Lincoln. It's all about personal development, Lincoln, personal development.

11 p.m.

Somehow I get to the Bankers' Party.

I can barely stand.

I think I'm standing tall as a Giant Redwood.

I almost fall over.

I'm pleased with how in control I look.

In between benders I've made many calls and The Club is full of bankers. The Boss is happy. Rik comes up to me and says:

—Great party, Linc. Can you get me eight girls in the booth?

I call the Floor Manager over. He sends eight Wraps into the booth with Rik, Steve and a couple of other Bankers I don't know. I hate not knowing Bankers. No one wastes more on Wraps than Bankers. I walk over to the booth and give them my card. They give me theirs.

On the main stage, three girls are dancing. Esurio is lying on the floor of the stage looking up in-between their legs. As they slide up and down the poles, he blows air up at their pussies. The Wraps look down to see where the air is coming from and one of them puts a stiletto straight through Esurio's forehead. I wince. Esurio smiles. The girls look puzzled and enjoy the air.

The Boss has a rule: *Never ask a girl to dance for you when you're in The Club. The girls are for the punters, not for you. Especially you, Lincoln.*

I don't like that rule, so I ignore it. One of the girls is stunning. When they have finished dancing, I ask her for a private dance in a booth next to the stage. As she spreads her legs I want to take my cock out.

The Boss has another rule: *Arms must be outstretched while the girls dance. Touching the girls is strictly forbidden and will result in immediate ejection from The Club. Especially you, Lincoln.*

I don't like that rule either. There are cameras in every booth. I scan the top of the booth until I find the one in mine. I turn and Esurio is beside me. He takes the handkerchief out of my jacket pocket and covers the camera:

—Now you can do what you want with her, Lincoln, anything you want ...

A few minutes later I'm standing at the bar talking to a Director of Consumer Affairs of one of the great British banks when I see Esurio tapping his jacket pocket and frowning. I try to ignore him. He gets even more agitated. I continue to ignore him until he strides up to the bar. He is furious.

—You're a disgrace, Lincoln!

—What the fuck are you talking about?

—This, Lincoln! This!

He stretches his hand out and prods my jacket pocket. I hate being prodded. I want to headbutt him. He doesn't care. Elegance matters more to him than personal safety.

—Your handkerchief, Lincoln, where is your handkerchief?

I look down. Fuck! I left it in the booth. He keeps going at me:

—How many times have I told you, in our line of work appearance is everything? You may be a wreck on the inside but it's the outside that matters, Lincoln, the outside. It's the outside that people believe in and, quite frankly, I'd be ashamed to be seen with you without a handkerchief. You have no pride. You might as well be naked.

In the early days, Esurio didn't even trust me to go shopping.

—You don't sell vans anymore, Lincoln. You're a *bon viveur* and you've got to look the part.

Once he knew he was going to be a big part of my life, he wrote this on a sheet of A4 and taped it to my bedroom door:

PRINCIPLES OF SARTORIAL ELEGANCE

1. A FINE DRESS SENSE IS THE KEY TO A LIFE OF EXCESS

2. PEOPLE HAVE NEITHER THE WILL NOR THE DESIRE TO SEE BEYOND APPEARANCES

3. IT IS BETTER TO BE POOR AND LOOK RICH THAN TO BE RICH AND LOOK POOR

4. WOMEN ARE EASILY SEDUCED AND LACK A CRITICAL FACULTY WHEN IT COMES TO MEN WITH A SENSE OF STYLE

5. ALWAYS WEAR A HANDKERCHIEF WITH A SUIT

6. IF YOU EVER DEGRADE YOURSELF BY BUYING CLOTHES FROM A HIGH STREET STORE ALWAYS REMOVE THE LABEL

7. CARRY A CANE OR WEAR A GARMENT THAT MAKES YOU STAND OUT SUCH AS A GOLDEN SHOE OR A FABULOUS HAT

8. A FINE SUIT WILL STAND IN YOUR PLACE WHEN AN EXCESS OF ALCOHOL HAS NECESSITATED YOUR ABSENCE

9. NEVER BUY A WATCH SIMPLY BECAUSE YOU WANT TO KNOW THE TIME

10. LIVE AND DIE BEFORE A MIRROR

Despite the fact that Esurio is a smug cunt and treats me like a fucking five-year-old, his Principles do the job, and I always get a better night's banging if at least a part of my day is spent before a mirror. It's not just the clothes. My grooming habits have become legendary in Soho. I go to a spa every week and I shave my chest at least once a fortnight. I wear designer perfumes, have chemical peels every month and dye my hair with particular care taken over the colour and density of my eyebrows. I have become obsessive about finding and plucking tiny hairs from pretty much every orifice, especially my nose and ears, and I've developed a habit of bending over, facing away from the mirror, and shaving every hair that dares to grow around my arse. I often blame Esurio for this, especially when the clippers catch a haemorrhoid, but the real cause is my compulsion to feed on Wraps: a hunger for pounding young pussy and an obsession with removing unwanted body hair go hand in hand.

I put my drink on the bar and am about to run over to the booth to get my handkerchief when David, the Floor Manager, comes walking over to me, hankie in hand.

—I can't prove what you did in there but you know the rules, Lincoln. No drugs in The Club. No sex in The Club. Not even any touching in The Club. You can play by your rules on the outside. In here, you play by The Boss's rules. And if you break The Boss's rules, he'll fuck you off whoever you are.

I am too ashamed to tell him I didn't break The Boss's rules, and I never will. Appearances are everything, so I say:

—Fuck you! I'll do what I want!

I grab my hankie, turn and go back to the bar. The Director of Consumer Affairs at a leading British bank is sniffing the air.

—There's definitely the smell of a really fine absinthe around here.

Esurio smiles at me and raises his glass. The Director is in his late sixties, moving his eyes and nose in search of the cause of his nostalgia.

—Haven't smelt one of those for years. A real vintage.

Esurio says:

—A man of impeccable taste. Actually, it's an Absinthe Jade 1901. One of the finest ever made.

I ignore him. Once he gets onto absinthe, he's like a broken fucking record. Absinthe La Maison Fontaine. Absinthe Edouard Pernod. Absinthe Capricious.

—*Capricieuse*, Lincoln, *Capricieuse!*

He knows them all. Yet whatever he puts in his mouth or up his nose he never seems to get hammered. Here's the evidence:

7 September 2009

I was with Esurio all night, except when I left him at the bar to go to the toilets three times to pound a Wrap. Because my memory is fucking horrendous I had a notebook with me to write down what he took. When I looked at the notebook in the morning I had written: eleven glasses of absinthe, two bottles of red wine, four liqueurs and four lines of coke. I made a note in the margin: perhaps it's three lines, because he insists the last line was snuff, whatever the fuck that is. I wrote some more but I was too pissed to spell, and part of the page is smeared because I think the Wrap wanked me off on it when I dropped the notebook on the toilet floor. By three in the morning I needed two extra sachets of Kamagra to get myself going with Suzie and a stripper from The Club, while Esurio was sitting stone cold sober in the corner reading a book. I fell asleep thinking he must be an alien.

12 September 2009

We went off to the cinema to see Lars von Trier's *Antichrist*.

—A bit of culture, Lincoln, while you can still see the screen and remember a storyline.

Before going, we had been getting hammered in the Soho Hotel until I threatened some guy who brushed against my shoulder as he walked past. Before we got thrown out, Esurio drank volumes of absinthe and three bottles of vintage Beaujolais. These are the notes I made after we left the cinema:

More absinthe. A gram of coke . . . she crushed his fucking cock and wanked him off until he came . . . blood . . . Another line of coke . . . then she cut her . . . off . . . two glasses of red wine . . . ant . . . re . . . . wi . . .

The last I saw of him was on the corner of Dean Street and

Old Compton Street looking up some bird's skirt who had drunk herself unconscious and was lying on the street.

—Good night, Lincoln. See you tomorrow. I'll stay here a while and admire the view.

I stop in the middle of the street. He is not even slightly drunk.

18 September 2009

This was one of my Paid-For nights. I started with a Thai Massage on Brewer Street – one of the best 'happy endings' I've ever had – then I went off to the Sanderson Hotel, where I met Sandra, one of the Wraps from The Club, three of her mates and a Paid-For. I annihilated them and, as I went from one arse to another, Esurio lay on the floor seeing how many bowler hats of red wine he could drink before I came. I counted four but, given the severe competition for my attention, there were probably more. When the Wraps had fucked off, he poured himself four large glasses of absinthe, laid them out on the bedroom table in a row, and drank them one after another in about thirty seconds before raising his hat to me and going out for an 'evening constitutional'. He walked like he had just had a good night's sleep and a glass of Evian.

I am sitting with Esurio in Starbucks on Wardour Street.

—Tell me, man, how do you fucking do it? Most nights I drink and snort more than you. I'm fitter than any bloke I know. I can shag for England. But I've never seen you pissed, let alone hammered.

—That would be telling, Lincoln.

—Fucking tell, then.

—Let me put it this way. My pleasure, Lincoln, albeit rather a vicarious one, is in sensing your pleasure. When you drink, it's like I'm drinking. When you snort, I feel the magic powder in my own nasal cavity, and the tiny part I play in your madness is better than the lead role in my own.

—Yeah, but what's that got to do with it?

—Everything, Lincoln. If I lose my mind I can't be there for you, and being there for you is what matters most to me. You're splendid entertainment and, in a way that you may never understand, you get hammered for both of us. You're more than a brother to me; you're my twin brother. You, Lincoln, are the debauched libertine I have waited all my life for and I'm not going to miss a second of it.

I think he's off his pampered head. I finish my Americano and leave for The Club. As I walk out of the door I shudder. I don't know why.

When I get to The Club, the Bankers' Party is descending into chaos. I look for Rik. When I can't find him, one of his staff tells me he's gone with the Director of Consumer Affairs to the Dirty Dance Strip Club. When I get there, he's sitting in a booth surrounded by Eastern European Wraps. There's about a dozen bottles of champagne on his table and he's waving wads of cash at the Wraps, offering every one of them two grand for a fuck.

—Why'd you leave The Club? The party's rocking.

—You can't get a fuck in The Club, or even ask for one, and what's the point in busting the country if you can't waste your customers' money doing whatever you want?

I pull the curtain and leave him to it. As I walk through the seated area next to the bar, I see the Director of Consumer Affairs slumped on a chair. Belinda, one of my Russian Occasionals, with great tits and an eye for a victim, is pouring champagne into a glass and forcing it down his mouth.

She says:

—Is good for you, Charles. Drink more, drink more.

He says:

—Uuuuhhhhh …

When I get close to them I notice a small packet popping out of her knickers. His eyes are bloodshot. He's slurring his speech and struggling to stay awake. His wallet is open on the table.

—What's in his drink?

—Champagne, Lincoln.

—Don't give me that shit. What's in his drink?

She pulls the packet out of her knickers.

—Fucking Rohypnol!

—So what?

I sense an opportunity.

—You can't do that, even in here. Give it to me or I'll tell your boss.

She throws the packet at me. As she walks off, she shouts over her shoulder:

—Since when have you started caring about rules?

The Director is asleep. I think how lucky the bank's customers are to have him on their side. Rik walks past with a stripper on each arm. He looks down at the sleeping Director and smiles:

—See, Lincoln, we're slowing down; this is the new face of responsible banking.

There are six Rohypnol tablets left. I take them all in one

go and finish the champagne. When I leave The Club I don't feel myself. I fall asleep in Bungalow 8. It's three in the afternoon when I wake up. Alone.

Nutella Nights

October 2009

I look at my watch: 15:55. I'm sitting on a table at the back of
The Office. My head is spinning. Drink. Coke. Cunt. Drink.
Coke. Cunt. Drink. Coke. Cunt. Drink. Coke. Cunt. I wipe
my hand across my lips. The Rioja tastes good. I'm on my
own. I catch my face in the mirror. I look. Empty. Fucking
Empty. The Office is a hub, a terminal I pass through at some
point every day. In a different place it might be a pleasant bar.
But it is not in a different place. It's in Soho and, like everything in Soho, it consumes its own customers.

Mario, the Manager, puts five glasses on my table and the
one next to it. He's nearly sixty and has been running The
Office for more than ten years. His profits are recycled in a
casino but he keeps smiling; he's the kind of man who would
be polished and polite on the gallows. Five glasses and two
bottles of Rioja. He's not clairvoyant. He just knows the
rhythm of alcoholics and, within a few minutes, I feel someone's hand wriggling my foot. I twist my face. I look up and
see Maynard, Terry, Simon and Steve. Maynard is sweating.
Thin, wiry, American and in his late forties, with a face so
gaunt it makes him look ten years older, he sweats most of the

time and always seems to be either on the verge of a heart attack or in the middle of having one.

Terry is tall with the kind of long hair that should have become extinct in the late sixties. He raises finance for films that never get made. He has knack of finding 'old money' that wants to rub shoulders with celebrity. The script is the same every time. First, he reels off the names of a few films he can remember when he's sober. Usually this works, except if he's hungover and his head is fucked. That's when he tends to go for the classics and that can cause problems. Like when he told an investor he helped fund *Citizen Kane*.

—But, Terry, you weren't even born when that was made.

—I'm sorry, not *that Citizen Kane*. I meant 'Kane' with a 'C' not a 'K'. Great art-house film made in the nineties.

—Oh, I see. Never heard of it myself.

—Well, you wouldn't have. Censors sent it underground. I'll get you a copy one day. Anyway, do you want to go to Cannes or not?

The Cannes close. Works every time. Especially for Terry. He gets to go to the Cannes Film Festival every year funded by some stupid cunt who thinks he's now bought into the film industry. To give Terry his due, he does know people in the industry and has good contacts in Cannes. It's just that he needs to borrow someone's crazy dream to get what he really wants: smashed. Preferably with a couple of East European escorts sitting on his face. He hasn't missed or paid for a festival in more than ten years. Hasn't made a film either.

Simon is a washed-up Yorkshireman who used to work a few Wraps until he became an 'agent', which basically means he puts adverts online and in shop windows around Soho and waits for Hopeful Girls to bite. I like the copy:

DO YOU WANT TO BE A FILM STAR?

Are you a young, attractive woman with real screen presence?

A leading Soho agent is holding auditions on xxxxxx for a new British thriller. If you want to work with some of the best names in cinema, call xxxxxx. Auditions will be held at xxxxxxx and filming begins in the summer.

Call now and take the first step on your road to stardom!

This is his sales pitch:

He photoshops pictures of himself next to some star or other and sticks them on the wall of an office he's rented for a week to conduct the auditions. He makes sure there are plenty of pictures of him on red carpets at Cannes or Leicester Square. These are real in the sense that he has a knack of diving under the ropes and getting Terry to take a picture before he gets kicked off. So when the Wraps turn up for their audition for a non-existent part in a non-existent film, they ask him lots of questions about what it's like to be on first name terms with Tom Cruise or Brad Pitt. He says:

—You can find out for yourself if you're successful.

Then they're putty. Numbers are exchanged and, within a few days, he's shagging them.

This is where Maynard comes in. Before he was chewed up by Soho he was a successful screenwriter in Hollywood. He's the real deal. When he shows a picture of himself with Leonardo di Caprio to some bird he's trying to shag, it's not a fake, and every now and then some A-lister flies into London and comes for dinner with him and the boys at The

Office. He arrived in Soho five years ago to work on a script he was writing and never left. Esurio loves Maynard:

—Nothing more elegant that true talent totally wasted, Lincoln. It's quite a delicious spectacle.

Then there's Steve, who hides under a thick mop of grey hair that falls onto his face. He's the quiet one, and even when he's snorting he's so fucking slow the only way I know he hasn't fallen into a coma is when I see a line wriggle its way up a ten pound note and into his right nostril. He was married once. Now all that's left of it is his mantra:

—I was never unfaithful to my wife.

At his own estimate, he's been sleeping with Paid-Fors every week for as long as he can remember, starting the week after his honeymoon. But for men that doesn't count as infidelity. Women never quite get this about men. Our brains are warehouses full of boxes. Some boxes are full of stuff, and some are so fucking empty they might as well be black holes. These boxes are sealed tight and live on different shelves. The 'Paid-For' box or the 'Porn' box never gets connected to the 'Wife' box, and that's how men build faithful marriages. Steve's wife kicked him out when she saw a picture on his phone of a Brazilian she-male sucking his cock. The best he could pull from his box of excuses was:

—Darling, I think I might be gay.

She believed him, kicked him out, and she still thinks that was his first and only indiscretion.

So the five of us are sitting in The Office and we are laughing. At thirty-seven, I'm the junior of the tribe but we all share an understanding. We are sick but never use that word. We are desperate but don't use that word either. We are drunk pretty much all of the time. But, above all, we are lost. We drifted into Soho and haven't the first idea how to get out. Of course, we have plans. Great films to be made. Beautiful women to fuck. Sunny beaches to lie on. But it is here, in this bar, stuffed with the scent of alcohol and aftershave, that we belong. Waiting for the next pussy or patsy to walk in through the door as the boxes gather dust and we struggle for air.

It's about midnight. I'm with Maynard in Little Italy on Frith Street. I am totally fucked. I need cunt. Now. I need cunt. Now. I need cunt. Now. I catch the eye of a young girl with a mass of dyed blonde hair standing in the far corner. I walk up to her. She says:

—Hi, I'm Melanie.

I find the direct approach works best. Blokes don't understand that women would rather share a strong man than have sole ownership of a weak one. I think:

—Be the Boss, Lincoln, be the Boss.

I sit down at the table, let her look deep into my coke-fuelled eyes, then I press my hand on her wrist and say:

—I really want to fuck you.

She can feel the strength in my hand. I can see shock and the hint of a smile in her face. She lingers too long before pulling away.

I lose track of time. It's probably about two in the morning and I'm with Melanie in the kitchen of my flat. Maynard is outside on the landing with Alison, trying everything he can remember to get the green light. He's sweating so much I think he's about to have a heart attack. He sways like a reed as the usual lines come out:

—I worked with Leonardo di Caprio, you know . . . Have you ever been to Hollywood? Do you know how the film industry works? I feel we have a real connection and I'd like to show you how to be really creative.

His short-term memory is fucked and, in a few minutes, he starts again:

—I worked with Leonardo di Caprio, you know ... Have you ever been to Hollywood?

Alison is maybe eighteen. She's a Hopeful Girl. She wants to be a film star. Maynard says:

—Fuck, fuck, where the fuck is it?

I pop my head around the kitchen door and Maynard is in my bedroom, looking for something in my drawers.

I whisper loudly:

—Maynard, what are you looking for?

—Fuck, fuck, where is it?

—What?

—That big vibrator. I need her to believe it's me.

—Try the third drawer.

He pulls out a pink Rabbit. Nine inches.

—Thanks, Linc.

I watch him for a few seconds. The logistics are too much for him. His drops the Rabbit and slumps against the wall. Alison falls on top of him. I go back into the kitchen with Melanie. We take a line off the kitchen table. I lie on the floor.

—Sit on my back.

Melanie hops on and I begin doing press-ups. I stop when I get to two hundred. As soon as I'm finished, I bend her over the sink. I want her arse. Now. Esurio is in the corner:

—Take it, Lincoln! Take it!

I try three times to get my cock in. I am bollocksed and her arse is too tight. She says:

—I've never done anal before.

I'm possessed. I look for some lube. The bedroom is across the landing. It's too far. I must get it in. I open the fridge door. Eggs, ham, half a pint of milk, cans of Budweiser, two bottles of vodka. Then I see it. Beautiful, brown and round. A jar of Nutella. I snatch it out of the fridge and open the top. It's almost full. I scrape it all out, one big dollop at a time. I'm sure I'm aiming for her arse, but I'm a child again and it's getting everywhere. By the time I'm finished her arse, buttocks, legs and lower back are all covered in Nutella. She is a Work of Art. Again she says:

—I've never done anal before.

Then she says:

—What are you doing?

I stand back for a moment, an artist admiring his canvas, before my cock ploughs through a Nutella mountain and into her arse. I am pounding when Maynard stumbles into the kitchen, sees the sticky brown substance all over her arse and begins throwing up. Melanie says:

—Is that someone being sick?

Then:

—I can smell chocolate.

Esurio is irritated:

—You could at least have used a better class of chocolate paste. Perhaps one from Fortnum and Mason. You've no class, Lincoln.

It must be morning. I'm in my bed with Melanie. My head hurts. The sheets and duvet cover are brown. I say:

—Fuck!

I put my finger on my arse.

Dry.

I put my finger on Melanie's arse.

Wet.

I pull my finger out and it has a brown lump on the end. I taste it.

—Better than I expected.

I can't see Esurio but I hear him shouting at me.

—Feed me, Lincoln, feed me.

I finish half a bottle of wine on the bedside table before getting up. Alison is unconscious on the landing. I look down and see a body on the stairs. I angle my head at forty-five degrees to improve my focus. It's Maynard. He is lying, feet facing up the stairs, one of his legs wrapped around the banister. I think he's naked. Then I see he has a sock hanging limp off one foot. His cock and balls are smeared in a pink liquid and a bottle of Johnson's Baby Lotion is lying by his side.

I shower and go for a run. About seven miles from Soho, up to the Heath and back.

I sprint all the way.

I feel my heart raging in my chest.

I outrun its anger.

By the afternoon Maynard is almost sober. I ask:

—So, what was all that fucking baby lotion about?

—Sorry, Linc. When I finally found my cock it wouldn't do anything.

—How exactly is baby lotion going to help?

—I think I went into the bathroom to look for some Viagra and all I could find was the pink bottle.

—But Maynard, it's fucking baby lotion.

—I know, but when I saw it I was too pissed to read the

label and I just thought: it's pink, it might be a special gay con-coction.

—A special gay concoction? What the fuck?

—Sorry.

7 a.m. The next day

I'm running across Hyde Park on my way from Soho to Kensington. It's one of those misty autumn mornings when I can actually hear the birds sing. My cock hurts from the night before and there's a pain stretching across my chest. I think I might die. I don't care. I'm three years younger than my father when he had his heart attack. I feel close to him. The pain across my chest gets more intense. I begin sprint-ing. One of us will have to surrender: me or the pain in my chest. After a few moments the pain begins to ease and, by the time I reach Kensington Palace and turn back towards Soho, my heart has settled into a calmer rhythm. I win. I need a drink. Some coke. A Wrap. When I get back to my flat there are a couple of Wraps crashed out in my bed. One of them is Melanie. I'm not sure who the other one is or how she got there. I'm as certain as I can be that she wasn't there when I left. But then I'm certain of nothing except that I need a drink and a line to steady me before I go to work. I take a shower and look in my wardrobe. It's full of dresses and female underwear, all between size zero and size ten. I think:

—How many girls are using your flat, Lincoln?

I guess it must be at least half-a-dozen Regulars and Occasionals. They have 'moved-in' with me, which means they pick up a spare set of my keys, which I leave in the drawer behind the bar at The Office, go to work then sleep, fuck and get hammered with me. We are all prisoners of Soho, and my room has become a sanctuary for the rootless, where we build a special kind of home, one fuck, one drink, one line at a time.

10 a.m.

I arrive on time. I'm always on time. I hold the handles of my office door. I need two hands to stop myself from falling over. The Boss is looking at me. I'm sweating. I think I should have taken another line and perhaps a couple more vodka tonics after my run to help me stand straight. Instead I'm leaning like a fucking cripple against the glass. I check my hankie is popping neatly out of my jacket pocket and smile across at The Boss. He smiles back. I think:

Great, he hasn't noticed.

He thinks:

The flash cunt will kill himself.

Once the meeting gets going I feel better. I am arguing with The Boss about two things:

- The Club is not a strip club. It's a Gentleman's Club.
- The videos on the big screens in The Club should not show the Wraps naked.

This is my reasoning:

- Big Spenders like to be referred to as Gentlemen. They can be the fattest, rudest cunts on the planet, but if they're going to waste a fortune on Wraps and champagne they want to do it in a Gentleman's Club, not a strip club. Even when their brains are back in the Stone Age, they want to take their status with them.

- Once the Gentlemen are in The Club, they need to be separated from their money. The most efficient way to do this is to use the promise of naked pussy to get them off the floor and into the booths for 'sit-downs' at four hundred quid an hour. Naked Wraps on the big screens are a barrier to this. They encourage wankers to stare all night at the screens and leave happy.

I win the first argument and lose the second. That's the thing with The Boss. If you want to win a battle you have to fight on more than one front, because there's no fucking way he'll settle for a dcfeat on aggregate. I'm good at my job and he likes me, which means I'm allowed a draw. After the meeting, he asks me to his office. While he rummages in his drawers, I look at his face. I am fascinated by him – the self-styled 'King of Clubs'. People take the piss. Not in Soho. Outsiders. The great and the fucking good. But he's better than all of them. He pulls out a picture of him standing on a beach. He's holding a piece of paper and smiling.

—Know what that is?

—Sorry, no.

—It's a notice telling me I'm skint. The day I was made bankrupt. I had nothing but the shirt on my back. Do you know how I did it?

—Wasn't it the clubs in America?

—That's how the story goes. The real reason is I thought I was invincible. Do you know how that feels?

I stare at him. He goes on:

—*You* know how that feels, Lincoln. But I wasn't invincible and neither are you. I lost my money. Then I got up off the floor and made more than I ever lost. You carry on like this and you'll lose your life and you can't get your life back. I don't know what you get up to in Soho, or who you do it with, but you won't be doing it much longer.

As I walk up the stairs to the ground floor of The Club, I'm crying, then I see Esurio sitting in one of the private booths. He is playing with a yo-yo. The sound of the string around the axle echoes through the empty club.

—Not getting a bit sentimental are we, Lincoln?

—Fuck off! Leave me alone.

—You know I can't do that, Lincoln. Especially when you're sad. All that matters to me is your happiness. I want you to have as much pleasure as you can. All the pleasure in the world, that's what I want for you, Lincoln, just like any true friend. I am a soulmate of your better nature and I want you to have more. Much more.

He lets the yo-yo rest in the palm of his hand and squeezes it. The silence is as dense as fog.

—The Boss is an old man, Lincoln. You're young. Everything is there for you. Reach out and take it. Feed me, Lincoln, feed me.

I know he's right. Of course, The Boss wants me to sort myself out. He wants to make sure I keep bringing in the bankers and the high rollers. But I know I can do that. Whatever I put up my nose or down my throat, I know I can do it. Esurio says:

—You're not like other men, Lincoln. You can take more and you deserve more. Why give it up now when we're having so much fun?

Esurio understands me. I *am* different. I'm a better class of loon. I can pound for England and run a half-marathon when I've drunk and snorted enough to put most guys into casualty. The boys in The Office call me a Legend and I think they are good judges of character.

As I walk out of The Club I think:

The Boss means well. I love him but Esurio *knows* me. When the time is right I will stop the madness. That time is not now. I have so much more living to do.

As I walk towards The Office I know the day is going to be extraordinary. I know it because there's a pattern. Here's how it goes:

1. The feeling begins in my gut. A spinning, twisting anticipation.
2. Once the feeling starts, I know three things: I am going to get bollocksed. I am going to get fucked. Nothing and no one can stop me.
3. I start smiling and wiping my lips.
4. I see images in my head: Drink. Coke. Cunt. Drink. Coke. Cunt.
5. I look at my reflection in the windows as I walk past. Sometimes I adjust my handkerchief. Other times I clench my fist.
6. I talk to any Wrap I fancy on the street. I always touch them. Usually on the arm or wrist before I speak. I say: *I love sex and I'm fucking good at it.* Or:

You're coming with me. Most of them take it because
they've fucked me before, know someone who has
fucked me, know that I am Lincoln and I fuck a
lot of Wraps, or because they are fucking terrified.

7. If I'm not fucking a Wrap by the time I get to The
    Office, I order two bottles of wine, a vodka tonic
    and take a line.

8. By now I'm a rabid dog and someone should
    section me.

9. I call a Wrap or one of them calls me. We meet at
    my flat, in a toilet somewhere in Soho, or I book a
    hotel for a few hours.

10. I spend the night believing in my own
    immortality while expecting to die at any minute.

3 p.m.

I'm in the Sanderson Hotel, sitting in the open-air bar waiting for Sandra. The tinkling of water from the fountains is
pissing me off. I go into the toilet and take a line. When she
arrives we go to the room. I rip her clothes off and tie her to
the bed. I go into the bathroom. I stare in the mirror and
begin twisting my face. My head is full of Wraps – fucked
harder than they have ever been fucked before. Esurio is
standing in the corner drinking some fucking absinthe.

—Let's eat, Lincoln!

I kick the door open, walk into the bedroom and kick a
coffee table over. Some plastic flowers and a few glasses crash
to the ground. I begin pounding her. I annihilate her. Women
pretend they want love and sometimes they do. But even

when they've found it, when they're knee-deep in nappies and anti-depressants, they also want to be fucked. Hard. So fucking hard they can't walk. Then they can go back to their husbands and love them. *Really* love them.

Most of the Wraps I fuck have 'boyfriends'. The trouble is boyfriends become husbands and husbands lose their power in a basket of dirty socks. I'm encouraged by the fact that evolution programmed women to want power and they know where to find it and when to take it. They have a nose for it. A sixth sense ripened over millennia. They know they'll find it when they go where other women go, and when I walk the streets in Soho I am always *armed* with women. The more women I'm seen with, the more women want to fuck me. Women say they dream about a white wedding and a faithful husband. Honest women say they dream about a white wedding, a faithful husband and another cock to fuck them senseless when the dirty socks start bursting out of the basket.

Esurio told me this once:

—The hunter who brings the carcass home is the one the ladies always go for, Lincoln. No one wants to go hungry, and men who kill are loved the most.

Sandra is screaming. The bed is bashing into the wall. Then it fucking breaks. The headboard cracks and one of the front legs snaps. She says:

—Don't stop, just keep going! Just keep going!

She thinks I want sex. I don't. I want to make a mark. I want her to remember me. Tell her friends. Think of me when she's holding her grandchildren and mourning her lost youth. I want to leave a cock-shaped footprint in her brain, deeper, more enduring, than any memory any man will ever leave there. Then I want to leave her. And I do. I always do.

I can't stop myself. It's nearly seven o'clock and she's lying on the bed. I've untied her. I look into her eyes. I see it there: a mark. Permanent. I have nothing more to say to her. I need a drink. I need a line. We smile at each other. I leave the room, pay the bill and by the time I've reached Oxford Street I've forgotten her. For a moment I know I'm a twat. I know it with greater clarity than I've ever known it before. I am ridiculous. A *poseur* playing a part. Not even an emperor without clothes. Just a naked actor. Esurio reads my mind. He walks alongside me:

—Ruminating again, Lincoln? Does you no good, you know, no good at all.

—What do you fucking suggest then?

—More, Lincoln, always more. It may be the only idea I have but I believe it to be a good one.

—How much more can I fucking take?

—Lincoln, you are in serious danger of disappointing me. There's always more. You know that better than anyone.

—I don't like admitting this but sometimes I get scared.

—Scared! What on earth is there to be scared of?

—Like when I don't know how to stop, or when that pain comes in my chest like it's going to explode.

—Trifles, Lincoln, mere trifles.

—You know what happened to my Dad.

—That's ancient history, Lincoln.

—They do say that early deaths can run in families.

—They? Who on earth are they?

—You know, experts, doctors, people like that.

—They know nothing about you. Nothing. They can reel off statistics but about you they know nothing. You want it. You can take it. So get on and do it. Life is a cauldron of pleasure and you bubble away happily in the heat. The more intense the better. Don't you agree?

—Yes, but I'm scared. I—

I look across at Esurio. He's gone. I look up and down Oxford Street. He's nowhere to be seen but I can still hear him. He's in my head. Going at me. He's fucking relentless. He never leaves me alone.

—More, Lincoln, more. Feed me, Lincoln, feed me . . . Hunger like you've never known Hunger before . . .

Then I see him outside the Archer Street Wine Bar. He smiles at me:

—Now, let's see how hungry you are . . .

I want to carry on walking. Just this once. To keep walking and find somewhere, anywhere, where he can't find me. I feel my stomach twisting, eating me from the inside out. I push open the door of the wine bar. Esurio has already lined up three vodka tonics. I drink the first one. He yelps with triumph. After each drink another one appears. It's an endless conveyor belt of alcohol until a man standing next to me touches my drink. When I'm on it I hate anything I own being touched by some clammy fucker. I especially hate my drink being touched. In seconds I have my hands around his throat. I can feel people pulling at my arms and jumping on my back. The man's face is going blue. He is losing consciousness. I know I am going to kill him and I want him to die. I want him to die and take me with him. Both of us. Together forever. Then I feel a thud on the side of my head and I collapse onto the floor. When I come round I'm lying outside on the street. Esurio is sitting beside me. He says:

—Much better, Lincoln. I feel like you're back to your old self. You see, it never pays to think too much. It's always easy to lose yourself in this idea or that. What matters is to live. Let me do the thinking for you.

I pick myself up off the floor and we walk into another Soho night.

Stairlift to Heaven

November 2009

Maynard and I are alone in The Office. He asks:

—What do you see in her?

—She's juicy and naughty.

—But she's in her mid-seventies.

—I like older women.

—But surely not *that* old.

I raise my eyebrows. The conversation is over. There is no reason I can ever give him to help him understand my love for older women. Especially *old* women. I tire of Wraps with their ridiculous hopes and designer handbags. There are times when I'm pounding them that I believe I really want them. But the truth is I don't. I feel lonely when I'm with them and you're never alone with a Granny. She is with you in the way a Wrap can never be. Decades of fucking, fantasy and frustration bring her to you complete: a woman who has lived, loved and lost; who has given everything to her children; who dotes on her grandchildren and who is trapped in a bubble of resentment and regret that only age can bring. She looks enviously at the Wraps, wanting one more, just one more, reminder of what it is to be young, to be *wanted*. Wraps have biology and fertility on their side but I would sacrifice all the Wraps I have ever fucked for a month locked in a hotel room with a Granny over seventy. A Granny like Ella. She says she is seventy-four, but I guess she's a few years north of seventy-five. Maynard says:

—But why waste your time with her?

—There's nothing like it.

He looks at me. The look a man might give his best friend when, after years of friendship, he discovers his friend is from another planet and they cannot understand each other. Esurio says:

—I love your appetites, Lincoln. They're deliciously perverse.

When I was barely a teenager I used to read a magazine called *Filthy Fifties*. It had a section called 'Vera's Veg Patch' where Vera would stuff an allotment of vegetables up her arse. Carrots, cucumbers, squashes, marrows – she got them all up there. Then I went to London on a school trip. To the Natural History Museum. While the other children looked at fossils I disappeared to Soho. It took me weeks to plan my trip to a sex shop. It was a feast my young senses could barely take in. The magazines I really wanted were on shelves I struggled to reach yet, as I raised my hands in hope, the magazines dropped down gently into my arms. Occasionally I saw the ghostly outline of some black gloves with only the wrist visible or the faint outline of a bowler hat. Sometimes a whisper:

—Enjoy it, Lincoln. You're young and everything you will ever want is waiting for you.

I didn't really understand what the whisper meant or where it was coming from. When I got to the counter a man said:

—You're too young, son. I can't serve you.

Then those spooky gloves and a smell of aniseed. The man looked confused. He said:

—OK, take them, piss off and don't come back again. You'll cost me my licence.

As I walked out of the shop, I heard the voice again:

—One day, Lincoln, one day we'll be best friends, you and I. The bestest of friends.

My Mum caught me wanking. All the time. She didn't mind the wanking. She did mind the *Gorgeous Grannies.* She said:

—It's not normal.

I didn't care. And I don't care what Maynard or any of the other boys say. A man who has never fucked an old woman has never lived. They say men want youth and beauty. I say:

—That's fucking fantastic! That leaves all the grey hair and saggy tits for me.

10 p.m. The Townhouse. Dean Street.

I can't keep my eyes off her. Maynard sees me looking.

—Quite nice, isn't she?

I'm puzzled.

—I didn't think you were into older women.

—You're not looking at the old one, are you? Please tell me you're not.

Of course I am. I noticed her as soon as I walked in. Even through the booze and the gear I couldn't miss her. I assume the woman with her, too old to be a Wrap, but still young, maybe mid-forties, is her daughter. The old woman gets up off her chair with the help of her daughter. I say to Maynard:

—Sixties or seventies?

—Seventies, I'd say. Early seventies.

—Yeah, I'd agree with that.

I catch her eye as she walks towards me. She knows, and because she knows, she presses her daughter's hand. She says:

—Maybe time for one more?

Her daughter pushes her cheeks out and exhales years of resentment. This is an old woman with attitude – the demanding, relentless kind who will outlive her grandchildren. I take her in. She has long grey hair, tinted with silver. Her face is well made-up. The subtle foundation contrasts with her lipstick, which is too deep a shade of red. I like too deep a shade of red. A colour that deep is always a betrayal and an invitation. The daughter says:

—You have to get back. You know that.

The old woman looks at her watch.

—I've got an hour yet.

—But what about your medication?

—It can wait.

—How many times do you have to be told? It can't wait.

I see Esurio standing behind them. He says:

—I feel a domestic brewing. Nothing whets a woman's appetite for rebellion more than a domestic.

I smile at him. The old woman says:

—If I say it can wait, then it can bloody well wait.

—But what about me? I've got to get home too.

—Oh, I thought it might be about you. Always about you, isn't it? One night out and you can't wait to get rid of me.

—One night? I've spent more nights than I care to remember running after you, pandering to your every need.

—Then go. I'll be just fine here.

She throws a half-smile in my direction. Esurio finishes a glass of vintage whisky and opens a half-bottle of Dornier-Tuller.

—We have lift-off, Lincoln.

The daughter snarls at the old woman.

—You're impossible! And so stubborn! Well I have to go and I will go.

She turns to Maynard, who happens to be the closest approximation to a responsible-looking middle-aged man that she can find around the bar.

—Please will you make sure she just gets in a taxi.

Maynard says:

—Y . . . Y . . . Yes. Er . . . what's her name?

—Fay.

Turning to Fay, he says:

—Don't worry, Fay. I'll get you home, wherever that is.

—It's a long way.

—Everywhere's easy from here.

Fay looks triumphantly at her daughter.

—Obviously not for some.

The daughter lowers her eyes, as Esurio raises his glass and says:

—Defeat is bad. Defeat coated in guilt is a prison of wretchedness.

Fay pretends not to notice as her daughter leaves and walks out into the night.

Maynard says:

—I promised I would get her home and I will.

I say nothing. I order another vodka tonic and turn to Fay.

—And what would you like?

Maynard says:

—Lincoln, I promised!

—And one for the considerate gent balancing on the bar stool.

Maynard puts his head in his left hand and keeps the right one extended. When I place a drink in his outstretched hand, the deal is done. Fay is mine. I will take her home. The next couple of hours are a blur but some detective work I do the next day tells me that our time at the Townhouse went something like this:

I leave Fay to go to the toilets.

I take three lines.

I come back.

Maynard falls off the bar stool.

No one can be bothered to lift him.

I feel sorry for him, so I pick him up and prop him against the bar.

Esurio says: Very noble, Lincoln. You are a true gentleman!

I drink two bottles of red wine and three bottles of Stella.

Fay has two glasses of red wine.

I notice she has a limp.

She says: It's nothing.

I think: I hope it doesn't get in the way.

Some Wraps are hanging around.

They want a drink.

They are invisible to me.

Esurio tries to look up Fay's dress.

He has to lie flat on the floor.

When he comes up he says: A true Victorian lady but with a twist, a real twist.

I think: I wish he'd fucking shut up.

Fay talks.

I don't hear what she is saying.

I go to the toilet and take another line.

When I come back Esurio is dancing on the tables.

He is beside himself with excitement.

He shouts across the bar: You are a man like no other, Lincoln, a man like no other!

I think: He's right.

I feel like the King of Soho.

I think Fay's lipstick is a bit smudged.

Then I'm unconscious for a while.

Two doormen carry me into a taxi.

They say: Good fucking riddance!

Esurio says: How rude! And to such a good customer.

The rest of the night I remember:

I open my eyes. I hear the rhythm of the taxi. Lights flash before my eyes. I feel sick. There is a hand on my thigh. I can't focus. I run my hands down a leg. It's covered in a dress. All the way to the floor. It can't be a Wrap. Then I see the lipstick. Fay. I run my hand through her grey hair and down onto her neck. As I knead the wrinkles, I feel better and my cock is hard. My vision is weird. I struggle to focus. The taxi stops. Fay says:

—It's OK, darling. Just follow me and be quiet.

I say:

—I really want to fuck you.

—Of course you do, darling.

She sounds like a nurse. I feel like a delusional sex addict on a psychiatric ward. I think:

—There is Truth in everything we feel.

When we get out of the taxi I make out some large, modern buildings. Fay says:

—You'll have to be very quiet.

I say:

—Of course.

I think:

Quiet! What is she fucking talking about?

We go in through a side door. I think:

—That's odd.

The lights are bright. I squint. I can see lots of doors. I say:

—You've got a really big house.

She looks confused. Then that nursey voice again, except this time it's slower and more deliberate, like she's talking to an adolescent with severe learning difficulties:

—Y–e–s i–t i–s, L–i–n–c–o–l–n. I–t i–s v–e–r–y b–i–g.

We go into her room. Then that switch goes on in my brain and I'm at it. I pound like a madman. She takes it like a gift she has waited years to receive. The bed vibrates and I can see her false teeth shaking inside her mouth, rising and falling in time with every thrust. After maybe an hour I notice how small the bed is. It's a single bed. I think:

—She must have thrown the double out when her husband died.

I'm a slave. I'm obsessed. I want her more than I have wanted any other woman. Her eyes glaze over. For a moment I think:

—I hope she's OK.

The moment passes and I forget. I forget everything. I'm lost in my own hunger. I hear Esurio shouting at me from the hallway outside:

—Feed me, Lincoln, feed me.

It goes on. And on. And on. When I'm done with her she says:

—Thank you.

These are the last words I hear before I fall into a deep sleep.

When I wake up, I feel sick. Fay is fast asleep. I have one foot in the bed, the other on the side rail and my head on the floor. I pull myself up using a metal grip protruding from the wall next to the bed for leverage. I think:

—That's handy.

I walk over to the bathroom. It's big. I press my hands against the wall for balance as I piss. When I'm done I look for the flush. I pull a red cord above my head. Within seconds the room is like a nightclub. Lights flash in the bathroom and an alarm rings so loud I think my head's going to explode. Red cord. Metal grips. I'm in a fucking care home!

Fay appears at the door. She is naked and looks like a granny doll with the stuffing taken out. I think:

—You are so fucking sexy!

I want her again but my head is spinning. She says:

—Lincoln, you need to get out now!

—Where?

—Through the window.

I rush out of the bathroom, fumble my clothes on and open the window. I turn to Fay:

—It's got restrainers on! I can't open it!

—Then force it open!

I bash it with my shoulder and fall out onto the grass. I think:

—Thank fuck we're on the ground floor.

She says:

—Run, Linc, run!

I sprint across the grass and, as I look back, I see two nurses rush into Fay's room. They see me on the grass. One of them shouts:

—Call the police! Call the police!

As I climb a wall onto the road, I look back and all I can see is Esurio riding a stairlift, faster than I ever thought a stairlift could move. He is going up and down the stairs at the end of the corridor using his cane as a riding crop. He is laughing hysterically and shouting at the top of his voice:

—*Ecce Homo*, Lincoln! Behold the Man! Behold the Man!

8 a.m.

I sprint back to my flat. There's a Wrap in my bed. I need a drink. I need a line. She says:

—You look like you've seen a ghost.

—I have.

—Where have you been?

—You wouldn't believe me if I told you.

—Nothing would surprise me about you, Lincoln. Nothing.

In an hour, I'm at The Club for a photo shoot. It's with twelve strippers for the 2010 calendar. I sit in one of the booths and watch the Wraps come in, one month at a time, one shaved pussy after another. I stare at them like I would a row of needy mannequins in a shop window. They disgust me. I disgust myself. I think of Fay. I wonder when her daughter will visit her again and what happened to her husband. If he's dead, was it cancer or a stroke or some senseless accident? Perhaps he just left her after decades of marriage, his last stand against his own inevitable decay. There seems so much sadness in the world, and I so want her to be safe and well it hurts. I whisper quietly into my coffee:

—Thank you, Fay, thank you, Fay, thank you, Fay.

I look up and Esurio is standing in front of me shaking his head.

—It's time to go now, Lincoln, time to go. I have something special lined up for you tonight.

I put the coffee down and leave the booth. I can still hear the camera clicking and the clunk of stilettos on the dance floor as Esurio opens the door for me and I walk into another day. By the time I'm on Wardour Street, Fay is a distant memory.

Midnight

I'm in a large warehouse in Soho and the cameras are rolling. There are about twenty beds dotted around the floor, a camera focused on each one of them. There's a naked Wrap on each bed with a sex toy in one hand and a phone in the other. Sometimes there are two or even three Wraps on one bed playing with each other. On the back wall are rows of neon numbers.

—What do those numbers mean?

Kevin, who runs the operation, replies:

—That's the number of callers listening.

This is the world of late-night sex chat for television. All the girls are being broadcast live on satellite and cable.

—Listening?

—Yep. That's how I make my money. For every caller talking to the girls, there's shitloads of dickheads just listening.

I look at the neon numbers. 17. 33. 42. 19. 57. I'm too fucked to count properly but by rounding up to the nearest ten I make it 420 listeners. Kevin passes me a pair of headphones.

—Here. This is what's happening on Bed Three. It's Danni, one of my top girls. One caller and you can see she's got more than seventy listeners right now.

I glance at Bed Three. I need to fuck Danni. Now. I put the headphones on. A man with a quiet, drawling voice, is talking:

—I like Tesco's best. The blue and white bags. The vegetables on the shelves. Especially the cucumbers.

—Ooh, darling, what do you like best about the cucumbers?

—They're long and they're Tesco cucumbers.

—Ooh, yes, and what would you do with a cucumber?

—Not a cucumber. A Tesco cucumber.

Danni may be the top girl but she's struggling with this one. Then she gets it:

—I bet you've touched a Tesco cucumber when you're in the supermarket and thought what you'd like to do with it, haven't you?

—Yes I have.

—And what's so special about Tesco cucumbers?

—It's putting it in the bag. I like sliding it in then dropping it so the bag makes a noise.

—Have you got a Tesco bag with you now, darling?

—Yes I have.

—Is there a cucumber in it?

—Yes, and I'm touching it now.

—Let me hear you move it in the bag.

A rustling sound shoots through my head. I am pissing myself laughing. I look up at the numbers. Listeners are now in three figures.

—I'm moving it around.

—Can you stroke it for me, baby?

—I'm stroking it now.

—Ooh, I bet that feels good, doesn't it. Stroke it harder for me, baby.

—I am, I am. Oh, oh, oh . . .

The line goes dead. Another happy customer. I have tears in my eyes and Kevin is cracking up next to me. When he sorts himself out, he points to the neon numbers:

—And that's how I make the money. One guy talks, hundreds listen and I want listeners not talkers.

—Why's that?

—Because talkers stop paying when the call ends while listeners stay on for hours. Cowardice costs money.

—How many of the models do you fuck?

—Hardly any. I'm so used to seeing naked girls it's about as much of a turn-on as a meeting with Mother Teresa. Probably less so. I even thought I was turning gay at one point.

I smile. I think he's insane.

I turn and see Esurio. He's lying on one of the beds helping two Wraps fuck each other with a dildo. They seem surprised at how well they're angling the dildo. He looks over at me:

—What a den of iniquity! This is what we want, Lincoln. Look at all the degenerate ladies. They're everywhere!

I watch him as he jumps from one bed to another. There's a blonde Wrap standing up on the corner bed and bending over, arse to camera. Esurio lies between her legs, running his fingers down her back. She shudders and wonders if the air-conditioning has been put on too cold. He moves like a ballerina using the beds as an improvised stage set. I go to the toilet and take four more lines. When I come out Esurio is running his fingers through Danni's hair. He has left me seven bottles of Stella on the chair I was sitting on.

—Now this is your favourite, isn't it?

Within an hour the bottles are gone and I'm staring at Danni. She goes off camera and walks towards the toilet. I follow her. I need her. More than I have ever needed anything in the world. I want her. I want to pound her. I can feel my guts twisting, gnawing at me, screaming at me. When I was about seven my Mum said to me:

—The thing about you, Lincoln, is that you always want what you haven't got and when you've had it you want something else.

When I was a teenager I was seeing a girl called Vicky. Her Mum said to me:

—I don't want you seeing my daughter anymore. There's something about you. It's in your eyes. They're all fiery. I just want her to go out with a normal boy because I know she'll never be happy with you.

Kevin is pissed off. He's banging on the cubicle door.

—I want her out of there now, Lincoln.

I don't ignore him because I can't even hear him. He has no idea how helpless I am. Then a door hits me on the back. I cling on to Danni with all my strength. I will not let her go. I feel hands. Four. Six. Perhaps more. Pulling me away from her and they carry me, my trousers around my ankles, to the fire exit and throw me out into a narrow alleyway. I slump against the wall. I think my cock is still out. There is litter everywhere and the smell of dog piss is so strong it finds its way through the barricade of alcohol and gear. Esurio is sitting next to me, looking up at the stars:

—What was it your hapless employer once said to you?

—Who?

—The one who said your fate was the gutter or the stars . . .

—Ah, my transport boss, Frank.

—That's the man. Lincoln. But you see, he was quite wrong. You can have them both. All you have to do is know where to find them.

Esurio gestures extravagantly, moving his arm from the alley to the sky and back down again.

—And I honestly believe we have found the perfect place.

The Next Day

I wake up and the left side of my face feels numb. I look in the mirror. There's a small cut and some swelling just above my jaw. It's just gone eight. I shower, put my tracksuit on, drop some cash in my pocket and go out for a run. The sky is grey. I sprint for the first three miles, then jog, then sprint. My chest begins to hurt. It clenches with fury. I am burning. I look at my hands as I run, waiting for the fire to break through my skin. I'm ecstatic at the thought of flames rising from my hands. Burning from the inside out. I don't know how far I run before the fire begins to cool. Perhaps nine or ten miles. I'm on Bond Street and I make my way towards Selfridges. I'm dripping with sweat. My eyes are like fucking saucers. I need a drink. I want to punch someone. I crave a confrontation. Two security guards standing at the entrance to Selfridges move towards me as I run towards them, then, as I get close enough for them to see the creature they are dealing with, they let me pass. I'm disappointed. I need a drink. My face hurts. I'm struggling for breath. I stop at the Gucci concession on the ground floor and lean against the wall. No one comes near me. I go to the toilets, throw up and wash my face. I put a toilet seat down and sit on it, my head in my hands. I want to rest. To be able to rest. I say:

—Five minutes. All I ask is for five minutes.

A voice from the next cubicle replies. I know it's Esurio:

—Now, you don't really want to rest, do you? It's a dangerous thing to rest. It's easy to get accustomed to a slower pace of life and we don't want that, do we, Lincoln?

—I just want five minutes then I'll be fine.

The tone of Esurio's voice becomes more insistent and I can hear his cane banging on the wall of the cubicle.

—No! I will not give you five minutes! Get out of here now and keep moving, Lincoln. Keep moving!

In seconds I'm at one of the cosmetics concessions. The woman serving me is the right side of fifty. She may even have turned sixty. Esurio is shouting across the shop floor:

—Don't ever think of slowing down again. So much opportunity and so little time. I will be your timekeeper, Lincoln, and my watch is a machine of perpetual motion. Perpetual, do you hear me? Perpetual!

I haven't a fucking clue what he is saying to me because my attention is locked like a missile on the woman trying various concealers on my skin.

—There. Perfect.

She pushes a mirror in front of my face. I can't see the cuts and the swelling seems less.

I've read about stalkers. I've even known people who have

been followed by them, but I never really understand them. What do they want? Why don't they give up? Why *can't* they give up?

After she finishes for the day, the woman on the cosmetics counter whose name is Sharon and who is, in fact, sixty-one, meets me at The Office. We fuck in three places. The toilets. Then my flat. Then the toilets again. When we're done she asks:

—When can we meet again?

I don't understand the depths behind the question. I say:

—Whenever you want.

—So, you're usually here, then, in The Office or at your flat?

—Sure. Or anywhere in Soho.

—Look, I need to know. I need you to be specific.

I'm sober enough to sense that what she's saying is odd. Esurio chips in before I get too suspicious:

—She wants you so much, Lincoln, she wants to know where you are *all* the time. That's your power over women. They just can't get enough of you. You are the Master!

I think:

—You're so fucking right! You know me better than I know myself.

So I give her my mobile number and I say:

—If you can't find me just call me and we can meet up whenever you want.

She smiles. I walk out onto the street knowing with absolute certainty that I am the King of Soho. I do not yet know that she is crazy. I get my first hint the next day. I'm going into a meeting with The Boss when I see a text from Sharon. It says:

—Where are you?

I think:

—I'll reply when I get out of the meeting. Always good to keep them waiting. Let them know who's Boss.

When I get out of the meeting I have over a hundred texts. All from her. Here's a small selection:

—Where are you?

—Where are you?

—I need to know. Where are you?

—Please don't ignore me. Just tell me where you are and we can meet up later.

—Are you trying to hurt me?

—Please, please, please, please, tell me where you are.

—I am not your toy. I deserve respect.

—I gave you everything.

—How can you do this to me?

—Do NOT NOT NOT NOT ignore me.

—I love you.

—I hate you.

—I want to hurt you.

—Sorry about the last text. I don't really want to hurt you. I just want to know where you are. I want to be with you.

—Fuck me, fuck me, fuck me, fuck me, fuck me.

—We are made for each other.

—Please fuck me.

—Don't you think we are made for each other?

—You will.

—If you won't tell me where you are, I'll find you.

—I'll find you.

—Bastard.

Esurio is looking over my shoulder and reading the texts with me.

—Got ourselves in a bit of a pickle, haven't we?

—What should I do?

—How am I supposed to know?

—You seem to know most things.

—Lincoln, I know how to make things *worse*. I'm afraid I'm not so good at making them better. Why don't you meet her and have some more fun? She's obviously a lady in need of more entertainment.

I think:

That's crazy!

Then I think:

Maybe he's right. Some 'Lincy Love' will sort her out. I can bang some sense into her.

Esurio says:

—You need to make sure you're fuelled when she comes round, Lincoln. Really fuelled.

After five hundred press-ups, two hundred crunches and a round of ridiculous weights, I leave the gym and I think:

My heart must be really strong. I can take anything!

When she arrives at my flat, she says:

—I need you. I want you. I love you. You can do anything you want to me.

So I do. I go mental on her. After three hours of pounding like a sewing machine, I have *marked* her. She will never forget me now. When I'm done she can't walk for a while, so I take the opportunity to say:

—Now we can both move on.

—What do you mean 'move on'?

—Well, you know, move on.

—But Lincoln, we're made for each other. You love me.

—Look . . .

I can't finish my sentence. I know I have just fuelled her madness with mine. I'm worried. And with good reason. Over the next couple of weeks this is what happens:

- She sends me shit-loads of texts every day. One of the nicer ones says she wants to cut off my cock and feed it to her pet dog.
- She follows me. I lose count of the amount of times I turn around and she's walking a short distance behind me. Sometimes she smiles. Not a nice smile. A snarly, haunted one. Other times she waves, like we're best friends meeting after a long absence.

Esurio says:

—At least you know what a stalker is now, Lincoln, and that was something you didn't know before you met Sharon. Like Tony Robbins says: it's what you *learn* that matters.

- When I go to The Club for business meetings, she waits outside. Sometimes she presses her face against the one-way glass, trying to look into The Club. Violet, the receptionist, gets a bit freaked out so she shouts through the glass:

—What do you want?
—I'm Lincoln's girlfriend and I'm waiting for him.
Violet tells her to go and sit in Pret across the road and wait for me there. When Sharon bangs on the glass a few times, Violet calls Security, and when I leave The Club after meeting

The Boss and George, Sharon is sitting in Pret smiling and waving at me to join her. I want to throw the stupid bitch under a bus but she is talking to a blonde barista called Marcia who I like. A lot.

Marcia: How's things, Lincoln? I like your new
    girlfriend. She says you're moving in together.
Lincoln:What are you talking about?
Sharon: *(touching my arm)* It's all right, love. No need
    to be shy. I told Marcia all about us and the
    wonderful places you've taken me.
Lincoln: What places? Old Compton Street? Just fuck
    off out of here!
Marcia: That's no way to talk to your girlfriend.
Lincoln: She's not my fucking girlfriend! She's a
    nutter!
Sharon: *(to Marcia)* He always says that. *(to me)* Not
    used to being in love yet, are you, sweetie?
Lincoln: We're not fucking in love! You're a loon!
Marcia: Come on, Lincoln, she's shown me the
    brochures.
Lincoln: What brochures?
Sharon: These darling.
*Sharon pulls out a handful of property details. Flats in and
    around Soho.*
Lincoln: That's not real! *(to Sharon)* And if you don't
    fuck off I'll get you locked up.
Customers are staring, sensing blood.
Marcia: Easy, Lincoln. Sharon said you were having
    some problems.
Lincoln: Problems? What fucking problems?

Sharon: I'm afraid I told her about the drugs and what the psychiatrist said.

Lincoln: What?!

Marcia: I think it's wonderful that Sharon's paying for your treatment. It will really help you get back on your feet.

I turn to face the counter, where Esurio is standing. He has a wicked laugh splattered all over his face.

Lincoln: (*to Esurio*) What are you laughing at? I need some help here ...

Sharon: (*to Marcia*) You see, like I said, he talks a lot to someone who's not there.

Marcia: Must be his imaginary friend. (*to me*) What's his name?

Lincoln: Esurio! And he's as real as you and me.

Sharon: Of course he is, darling. Now I think it's time to leave.

Sharon and Marcia exchange a knowing look. I kick the door and make my way to The Office *leaving Sharon standing at the top of the street.*

Sharon: I love you! I love you! I love you!

* Sharon freaks out the Wraps. She stands outside my flat screaming:

—Shag me, shag me, please shag me!

One of the Wraps lets her in and she keeps banging her head against my bedroom door. The Wrap sends me a text saying:

Your crazy girlfriend is banging her head against your bedroom door. I gave her some coke to help calm her down. She's begging you to fuck her. Should I call the police or are you coming round to shag her?

I text back:

She's not my fucking girlfriend and don't even think about calling the police. I'll be round in five minutes.

A few seconds later I text again:

And I'm not going to shag her.

Then she disappears out of my life. The first thing I notice is that I haven't had a text for half an hour, then an hour, then a whole day. After a couple of days I get a call from an *Unknown* number. *Unknown* has lost its appeal to me. It is tainted with fear. I answer it. A man says:

—Hello, Lincoln?

—Who's that?

—David. Sharon's son.

—Yeah?

—I would just like to apologise for my mother. She's not well. I'm taking her back to Cornwall. She won't bother you again.

Esurio says:

—Now it all makes perfect sense. *Cornwall.*

—What do you mean?

—Not our kind of madness, Lincoln. Cornwall is full of druids, temple bells, angels, fairies, spirit-channelling and healing with hieroglyphics. A blight on the face of the earth, if you ask me.

I don't know what he's talking about. I take a line and open a bottle of Rioja. Within minutes I'm dreaming of the next Wrap and Sharon is already a distant memory.

A Magical Christmas

Esurio is like an excited five-year-old.

—I adore Christmas, Lincoln, adore it.

He's making some notes in a fancy snakeskin notebook.

—What are you writing?

—I'm not writing. I'm planning!

—What are you planning then?

—I'm planning a special Christmas for us, Lincoln.

—Like what?

—I don't know for certain yet, that's why I'm planning.

—Well, give me a fucking clue . . .

—OK. These are only ideas, you understand. Very rough outpourings of my imagination. But I do think you will like them.

—Try me.

—Well, it's fair to say in recent years your Christmases have been a bit disappointing. I agree that you did your best to throw up over the Christmas turkey last year but that was down to a tummy bug rather than any excess of your own doing. And the years before, well, there were a few parties here and there but nothing to satisfy a man like me. But now things are different. This is our first *Soho* Christmas and we have to make the most of it. You don't know if it will be our last.

—Well, it's not going to be our last, is it? I intend to stay here a long time.

—I don't deny your intention, Lincoln, but Soho isn't like that, is it? You may *intend* to stay but then, one sunny day, it's one tipple too many and you've gone to the Big Bar in the Sky.

—Thanks for your optimism.

—My pleasure. Now listen to this. It may help you on your way. I've called it *Esurio's Magical Christmas.*

—Fucking get on with it.

—OK. During the Merry Month of December, Lincoln will aim to surpass all previous achievements in his life by undertaking some very tricky challenges. To date, I have enumerated three and I believe they will suffice. First: to inseminate at least fifty ladies. These can be young or old, free or paid for. It's the number that counts. Second: to consume more cocaine and alcohol in a single day than he has ever consumed before.

—Excuse me, how am I going to know when I've done that? I've no idea what's the most I've ever taken. I'm always too bollocksed to count.

—I've thought of that, so I've made rough calculations based on my own observations and using, if you don't mind me saying so, a slightly more functional memory.

Esurio shows me some workings-out on a page that look like an accountant's spreadsheet.

—I don't understand them.

—You don't need to. I wouldn't want you to waste your time thinking when there's so much doing to be done. When I've completed my calculations I will simply give you a list and you will act on it.

Esurio lifts his pencil off the page and waves it in the air:

—Last, and by no means least, he must become the proprietor of his own nightclub.

—What the fuck?

—I know it sounds rather improbable but I feel you are sometimes held back by not being your own boss. Imagine what you could do if you owned a club and all the alcohol and women were at your disposal whenever you wanted them. I really feel you deserve this opportunity, Lincoln. You have worked hard all your life and you are more than capable of running a business.

It's only mid-afternoon but I'm already unsteady on my feet, my head feels a bit fuzzy and I can't think straight but, after a few seconds of careful reflection, I say:

—Do you know, I really think you've hit on something there. I've got so many ideas. Things I'd like to do with the bar, what the girls would be wearing, the carpets and lighting.

—Splendid!

I'm lying. All I'm thinking about is pussy. I imagine Wraps on the first floor and Grannies on the second. I say out loud:

—It'll need to have a lift.

—What?

—Oh, nothing. I'll have the Grannies on the ground floor and that'll solve the problem.

—I have no idea what you're talking about. What matters, Lincoln, is your business acumen, not your recently discovered talent as an architect.

He's right. I have run businesses in the past and it's fair to say that my success as a Sales Director has not been matched when I take on more general responsibility for a business.

This is the problem: I'm aware that businesses need structure and I'm an animal that's better contained under the direction of others. I am certainly not a man you would ask to build his own cage.

Here, in what I believe to be the correct sequence of events, is what happened the last time I owned a share of a business:

I was known in the transport industry as the best Sales Director in the UK. I was also known as a nutter. Not a drinker in those days. Just a man with a terrifying temper shorter than a gnat's cock. A successful businessman called Gerry asked me to be the junior partner in a new venture he was setting up in the marine industry. I agreed. He was minted and I soon learned why. When we travelled we shared a bed in cheap hotels to save money. He always had a jar of Vaseline with him, which he would rub on his cock and wank while I was trying to sleep. I got his business moving. I sold pretty much every lead I went on. He said:

—I couldn't do this without you. You're the best salesman I've ever worked with.

When we were in a café in Berlin he said something to me I didn't like. I threatened him. He hit me. He really shouldn't have hit me. I chased him down the road. He was knackered after a few hundred yards. I caught him, sat on him and used his head as a punchbag. His life was saved when some men managed to pull me off.

Gerry's wife was worried about my temper. She told him to say this to me:

—You can sell but you can't manage. This business is better without you. You're out.

Gerry did as he was told. We were in a restaurant when he

broke the news. I threw a table on its side and ran out. If I had stayed I would have killed him. He was grateful I didn't kill him and, years later when we met, he said:

—Thank you for not killing me. You're a great guy, Lincoln, and you could sell condoms to the Pope but never try to run a business.

I said:

—You're right. I won't. I promise you now I'll never try to run a business.

So I say to Esurio:

—I'll call the business *Townleys.*

—Not very original but it's your business and you can do whatever you want.

—You're right. Whatever *I* want.

December proves to be sensational. I pass the first challenge a week before Christmas. Then I do something really fucking stupid. I try to pass the second and third challenges on the same day. The same fucking day. Which is also the day of the Sexy Santa Party at The Club.

8 a.m. The same fucking day. Which is also the day of the Sexy Santa Party at The Club

I've been awake for an hour. I'm in reflective mood. For once I'm alone in my bed. I was hammered yesterday but less so than usual. I was preparing myself for today. I go out for a run. Westminster is beautiful in the hazy winter sunshine. I'm feeling good. I smile at people as I run. The streets seem strangely calm and meaningful, as if I might actually accomplish something on them. In this moment I am certain only of my own success. I've arranged a meeting at a private members' club in Kensington for ten o'clock tonight. Inside every drunk is a tale of missed opportunity and I am determined not to miss this one. I spoke to Rik and some of his banking friends and they're interested in backing me if the current leaseholders allow me to take The Club over:

—We know you can get the best girls, so if it's got a fully nude licence then we'll definitely consider backing you.

—Of course it's got a fully nude licence.

It hasn't got a fully nude licence, but this is my Big Chance and I'll do anything to make it happen. The fully nude licence is just a detail I'll sort out later. Gerry used to say:

—Business is about small details. The more boring your day, the better your business.

My problem is that I'm not so good at details. I believe:

—Business is about selling and, if you can sell enough stuff, the details will look after themselves. Business should be exciting.

I've arranged to meet Rik at the Sexy Santa Party about midnight, once I've gone over to Kensington and had a look. I have chosen today to drink and snort more than I have ever drunk and snorted before because I want to prove a point. When I told Esurio that I was doing the second and third challenges on the same fucking day, I said:

—I want to show everyone that I can handle the booze and the gear, that I can close a deal with half of Colombia up my nose and perform better when my guts are like a distillery than most men can when they're sober.

—That's a very noble ideal, Lincoln, and one that I am fully supportive of. We both know how good you are, whatever state you're in, and now is your chance to really prove that to the world.

So that's why I feel so good sprinting around Westminster. I think I've run about six miles but I feel like I can go on forever. I feel Immense. Immortal. I stop off at the gym on my way back to the flat and hammer the weights and the treadmill for just over an hour. When I'm finished I'm a ball of sweat.

At the flat Esurio is waiting for me. He has a list in his hand.

—This is what I believe you need to take today to pass the second challenge. The day is not a day as normal people understand a day to be. This day ends, Lincoln, when you either fall asleep or collapse.

This is what the list says:

5 bottles of wine. Vintage is preferred but any wine will do.
A minimum of 10 vodka tonics.
A minimum of 20 shots.
5 bottles of Stella.
5 grams of cocaine.
10 cups of coffee. Preferably Americanos.
2 inseminations. The ladies are at your discretion.

Esurio continues:

—I realise that you will be in no state to keep a check of your progress, so I will do that for you. You can be totally confident that I will be fair and scrupulous in my counting. Off we go, then!

I begin in my room with a line of coke, a bottle of Stella and half a bottle of wine. This is the day my life changes. More madness than ever before *and* my own nightclub. I am euphoric.

11 a.m.

The Boss, George, Jack, Mark and I are in an office at The Club. I look at a photograph from the 1970s of The Boss and Mick Jagger. George is talking. I'm not listening. He knows I'm not listening, so he asks:

—What do you think, Lincoln?

—I think it will be a great party. Best Christmas party ever. I've got all the City boys coming and I've been hounding all the concierges at the five-star hotels to recommend us to their punters.

—That's great, Lincoln, but we weren't talking about tonight. I was asking for your opinion on whether we should change the house champagne.

The Boss looks at me. He is not happy:

—Are you in this meeting or not?

—Sorry, Boss.

—You look hammered and it's only just gone eleven.

—Give me a break. I've got a lot going on today.

—I'm always giving you breaks. So now that you've brought tonight up, what do you think we'll take?

—I think we'll break all records. I know you don't like tipping the concierges.

—Too right. Everyone knows The Club. Where else are they going to send the punters?

—Platinum Lace, For Your Eyes Only, Sophisticats, Spearmint ...

—Are you being smart?

—No, but some clubs pay the concierges and we don't, so this time I've printed the leaflets and, for every one we collect at the door, I'll personally pay them twenty quid a punter from my own pocket.

—I don't like it, Lincoln.

George chips in:

—If he remembers to do it and hasn't stuffed his money up his nose.

The Boss throws a look at George, who backs off. I continue:

—I promise we'll hit target. I've been on my phone all week and I know the boys are all coming. It's going to be massive.

3 p.m.

I take some Kamagra. I am about to 'inseminate my second lady of the day' in the toilets at The Office and without the magic gel I haven't got a prayer. When I'm done, Esurio is waiting for me at a table in the corner.

—How am I doing?

—Very well, Lincoln. I expect you to pass with flying colours.

I feel sick. I clench my teeth and wipe my hand across my mouth. I have two bottles of Rioja and three vodka tonics on the table. My phone rings. It's Rik:

—All on for tonight, Lincoln?

—Of course.

Esurio can see I'm struggling, so he says:

—Keep going, Lincoln. You never give up, do you?

—No. Never.

8 p.m.

I can barely walk in a straight line. I'm ecstatic. I'm going to run my own nightclub.

10 p.m.

As I walk up the steps of the club in Kensington, I stop and look up at the stucco-fronted four-storey Georgian house. I am with Maynard and a Wrap called Mia. The house is moving. I struggle to focus. There are two doormen at the top of the steps. They look at me. It's obvious they don't know who I am. I say:

—Good evening, you probably know who I am. I'm Lincoln Townley. Your boss is expecting me for a meeting. I'm going to be taking over this club.

I think they look at each other but I can't be sure because I can't see straight. The bigger of the two doormen steps forward.

—Are you sure, sir?

I take a step towards him. I stumble. He grabs me by the arm to stop me from falling. I shout at him:

—Let go of me now!

He does. I fall. I say again:

—I'm Lincoln Townley. I'm here for a meeting with your boss.

One of the doormen goes inside. In a few moments he comes out with a tall man dressed in a smart casual jacket. He is languid and has the kind of quiet presence you never mess with. I ask:

—Who are you?

—I'm Luigi, the manager of this club. And you are?

—Lincoln Townley. I have a meeting with the owner about me taking over the club.

Mia and Maynard are holding one arm each to keep me vertical. Luigi is polite.

—I'm sorry, but Mr Green is not here this evening. Can you come back another day?

I wonder who I made the appointment with. It was with a man I met in the Townhouse. We were both drunk. He said it was his club but his name wasn't Green. I don't give anything away.

—Sorry, my backers are expecting a report from me and I need to look around inside.

Luigi says nothing. He gestures me to come in. If I was sober I would have been gobsmacked that he let me in. Under the circumstances I simply believe it is the respect I should be given as the future owner of this club.

Inside the club is tired. There's a bar and a lounge area on the ground floor. Luigi offers us all a drink. I notice one of the doormen is standing close to us. I ask where the toilet is. I piss and take another three lines. By the time I'm back at my table there's a vodka tonic waiting for me. I down it in one. I walk down a narrow flight of stairs to the basement. I'm doing fine until I miss the last step. One of the bar staff who happens to be standing at the bottom of the stairs catches me. I can hear Esurio:

—You're doing splendidly, Lincoln.

—I know, I know.

I turn to Mia and say:

—I want another line.

She says:

—No more. You've had enough.

—Enough! Of course I haven't had enough. There's always more. I'm going to take another line whether you like it or not.

She starts crying. I ignore her. She storms out of the club. Later on I learn that she went back to her flat, packed her stuff and took a flight back to Denmark. When I get back to my table on the ground floor I order another drink. I say to Maynard:

—I could make a proper go of this. This whole place needs freshening up and I'm the man to do it. Rik knows how good I am. I'll sell this to him.

1 a.m.

I don't know how I got back to The Club but I am here. The place is heaving. The Boss is sitting on his throne in the restaurant. I go up to him:

—You see. The Club is bursting.

He leans towards me.

—Yes, it is. Now take a look at it and imagine what you could do if you were sober.

I think:

—It makes no difference whether I'm drunk or sober.

I feel sorry for The Boss that he can't see this, but out of respect I say:

—Yeah.

I walk downstairs and see Rik with two dancers, one on each lap. I say:

—It went well.

—What?

—The visit to the club.

—What club?

—The one in Kensington.

—Oh, yes, of course, that club.

—I think they were really impressed with me.

He's not even looking at me. His eyes are full of tits. I continue:

—If we make a few alterations to the layout and fill it with girls, it could work brilliantly.

—I like the bit about filling it with girls.

—And naked grannies.   ·

—What?

He doesn't get grannies the way I do. I change tack.

—And naked fannies.

—Yeah, even more brilliant. You're a helluva guy, Lincoln. A man worth busting the banks for. Cheers!

—Cheers!

I walk towards the stairs to go back up to talk to The Boss when everything folds in on itself and The Club is twisting and a carousel of lights, sound and naked female flesh spin before my eyes. I hear voices, laughing, screaming, crying, and my heart is pounding like a wild beast roaring inside my chest. I need a drink. I need a line. I need them more than I have ever needed them before. I'm dying. I want to die. I want all this madness to end and I want it to go on forever and ever and everything is fading and coming back, fading and coming back. My legs are paralysed and I'm running faster than I have ever run before. I'm standing on top of the highest building in the world and grovelling about in the dark in a deep pit and there are people with me. I don't know who they are and they're laughing at me, spitting on me, honouring me as their god. There are caravans and dead fathers and smashed-up toys and blood lying on the road and music keeps banging inside my head and Wraps are everywhere. I'm lost in a dark forest and running along deserted beaches and swimming in rivers that wind endlessly on and I can hear Esurio. He is mocking me: *You're mine now, Lincoln, mine. There is no way out now, Lincoln; you can never get away from me. We are friends forever.* And he's leading me to a tall cliff. I have chains around my hands and feet and a metal collar around my neck, and he is pulling me closer to the edge. I look over and I know this is the end. There is no way back now. I lower my head. I am tired beyond exhaustion. Spent. The last thing I see is the vast ocean pulling and twisting in its own fury. Calling me. Esurio releases me. He knows I have no need to be pushed. I want to lose myself without hope of ever finding myself again and I step over the edge. I can see Esurio laughing and dancing as I fall into the sea. He watches me sink down deep and it is so peaceful under the water. Dark. Dark. Dark. I know I can rest now. It is over. I am carried far out to sea and in the deepest dark I see lights, ghosts that have swum here for centuries, and they are stroking my body and whispering to me: *Rest now, Lincoln, Rest now, Lincoln, Rest now, Lincoln . . .*

4 a.m.

I collapse at the bottom of the stairs. David, the Floor Manager and one of the doormen put me on a stretcher and carry me upstairs. I have a vague sensation of cold air on my face as I'm carried out onto the street. They drop me off the stretcher and prop me up, legs extending out onto the pavement. I can hear The Boss's voice:

—Just leave him there. He can sleep it off on the street. What a mess.

Someone takes my hankie out of my jacket pocket and places it gently on my face. I am unconscious within seconds.

6:30 a.m.

Sound comes first. Cars. Cutlery jangling in a cafe. Footsteps. A babble of conversation. Nothing is defined. It's just a reassuring buzz around my head. Slowly I open my eyes. Even the morning light is too strong. I can feel a hand lightly tapping my left cheek. Esurio is talking to me:

—Well done, Lincoln! Congratulations! You passed with flying colours. I've checked my list and you've surpassed yourself.

I groan. I try to raise my arms but my hands flop back against my body. I can feel a wet sensation on my shirt and jacket. Esurio says:

—Don't worry about that. We can get it all dry-cleaned.

—Why? What is it?

—I'm afraid someone urinated on you during the night. Not very gentlemanly, I agree, but I assure you it will clean up perfectly well.

I put my hand inside my jacket. My phone and wallet are still there. I feel sick. Sicker than I've ever felt in my life. Esurio goes on:

—I'm not going to make a big issue about the club.

—What club?

—The one you went to see last night in Kensington.

—Oh yeah. Do I own it yet?

—Not exactly, but I've given you lots of marks for effort and you've definitely laid some solid foundations, Lincoln, very solid foundations, and you've done so well on the other challenges it would be churlish to mark you down on this one.

Then he's gone. After a few minutes I pick myself up off the floor and make the short walk back to my flat on Old Compton Street. Every step hurts. I fumble my key in the door. Focus, Lincoln, focus. When I get up the stairs and into my room there are two people in my bed. One of them is a Wrap and the other one is . . . Rik! He looks up at me:

—Hope you don't mind, Linc. We hit it off and she said she had a key to a flat. Didn't realise it was yours.

—No problem, man.

And it really isn't a problem. I don't care anymore. About anything. I grab my running kit from the wardrobe. But for once even I am too tired. Too tired to run. I shower, change, turn left out of my flat and just keep walking. My phone is buzzing with texts and calls. One of the texts is from The Boss. He writes:

—I hope you're OK.

I reply:

—Better, thanks. I'm out for a walk. Sorry about last night.

—I'm glad you're OK but don't ever turn up at The Club in that state again. Never ever.

—I won't.

Then:

—Keep it real. Just keep it real.

As I walk through the early morning traffic, I have no idea what is real in my life anymore. Dean Street, Wardour Street, Brewer Street, Frith Street, Greek Street and all the alleys and dark corners of Soho. These are fantasy streets. Places where imaginary people get lost chasing dreams they can never find. I pass an art shop on Broadwick Street. I stare through the window.

—Keep it real. Just keep it real.

I think again of my favourite painting, *A Bigger Splash*; all that serenity on the surface and a ferocious struggle going on under the water. And who or what is struggling?

Cars, bikes and people pass me by. All of them going somewhere, doing something, and I'm floating past them, no idea why I am walking these streets, watching reality fade in and out of life like a flickering TV picture.

9 a.m.

I wander into Foyles bookshop on Charing Cross Road. I'm looking for a book about Hockney. I find a book by Paul McKenna. *Change your Life in 7 Days*. That doesn't seem too difficult. It's Friday. A Brand New Life by next Thursday. I look at McKenna's face on the cover. A Geek with Glasses. I feel an urge to smack him in the mouth. I don't buy the book. I don't need to. 7 Days. Change my life. How difficult can that be?

How Difficult Can That Be?

The First Day

I think:

—I don't need the book. It's the Principle that matters. If a Geek with Glasses can change his life in seven days, so can I.

After leaving Foyles, I go to an art shop on Berwick Street. When I leave, Esurio is following me.

— What are you doing with that box of paints, brushes and a canvas?

—What do you think?

—I am, as you know, an art lover. Nothing moves me like a standing in front of *The Satire of the Debauched Revelers* or *The Garden of Earthly Delights*. I have actually cried tears of joy when looking at *Three Studies for Figures at the Base of a Crucifixion*. But I feel that painting is not the correct thing for you to be doing right now.

—Why not?

—I saw you in the bookshop looking at that 'change your life' nonsense, and if painting is the first step on this new path of yours, Lincoln, it won't work.

—You sure about that?

—Of course. Why on earth do you want to change when you are only now beginning to lose yourself in the pleasures you have worked so hard to enjoy? And it was only yesterday that you achieved so much in passing what were extraordinarily difficult challenges.

—But I nearly fucking died. And I woke up covered in piss.

—As far as I can see, you're alive now, and there's plenty of dry-cleaners in Soho. And who, I ask you, was at your side when you woke up? Me, Lincoln. And who will always be at your side? Me again. I understand you, Lincoln, and I know what's best for you. The last thing you need is a self-help guru when you have me. Am I not enough?

—Enough? You're too fucking much.

—I'll take that as a compliment. I know that artists have a long history of abusing their nervous systems in the service of creativity, but I fear that your impulse is rather different. You just want a break.

—Yeah, I do. I want seven days of doing something different, when I don't wake up sweating, full of anxiety, waiting for my heart to explode.

—A break, Lincoln, can extend from days into weeks and months, perhaps even years. When you're on a roll it's always best to keep going. Breaks mess up an established routine and can, in tragic circumstances, alter it permanently and you wouldn't want to stop drinking and using, would you?

—Not permanently, but maybe for a week.

—And what *reason* do you have to stop?

I look at him. He smiles. We both know I don't have an answer.

Apart from the magic seven days, all I remember about the book was the title of the first chapter: *Who Are You Really?* I haven't a fucking clue who I am, what I'm doing or where I'm going, so my job for the First Day is to fill in at least some of those blanks. Here's the result of my best efforts:

I Really Am:

A Cunt
An Alcoholic
A Coke Freak
A Pounder of Wraps and Grannies
A Great Salesman
A Ball of Muscle and Anger
A Father
A Son
An Artist

When he sees the list, Esurio can't help himself:

—You see, Lincoln, where does honesty get you?

—At least it gets me a list.

—So choose one, then. My choice would be the first item on the list. Absolutely you in one little word.

I want to be a Father or a Son but I lack courage, so I go with the next best thing:

—And mine is the last and that's what I'm going with.

When I get to the flat I prop the canvas on the dressing table and begin painting. I feel sick and I need a drink. Every stroke of my brush is an effort until, one slow movement at a time, I disappear into what I'm doing. The twisting in my stomach eases and I become the rhythm of my brush on the canvas.

I am a child again. I feel breathing behind my left shoulder. I turn and my Granddad Bob is watching me:

—Hold it this way, Lincoln ... That's it ... Picture what

you want to do and let it happen ... There's no right or wrong ... Just enjoy doing it ...

I can feel his hand holding mine as it moves.

There were paintings on the wall of our council house when I was growing up; all of them given to us by my Granddad. He was an engineer; a short, stocky man who worked in an artillery factory during the war, and he was as hard as the shell cases he made. He was also skilled at re-engineering the human body. Someone threw a dart in his head once and before he could say *One-Hundred-and-Eighteeeee*, the guy who threw it had his nose moved to the side of his face, like a Picasso. The rules were simple: you cross Granddad Bob, you pay a price. One of his favourite sayings was:

—They all pay. One way or another they all pay in the end.

He developed a variation of that saying for me:

—It doesn't matter whether you're in a brothel with a prostitute or a church getting married, you always pay for it one way or another.

Bob was one of those men who surprised you. Just when you thought you knew 'his type', you found something out which made you question whether he really was 'his type' at all. As well as keeping the long-standing Townley tradition, passed down the male line, of throwing a killer right hook, he was a talented artist. He didn't just give us the paintings on our wall. He painted them and he kept painting until he began to lose his mind, and that's when he forgot much more than how to paint. He forgot who he was. Where he lived. Everything.

When the Alzheimer's got bad he could no longer live on his own. He had nowhere to go, so I moved him into my flat in London. His memory came and went in waves. One day I came home and he was sat in the garden with a sketchpad and some pencils.

—What are you drawing?

—A lake and some trees.

—Yeah, I can see it. It's beautiful.

It was just a random series of lines and colours. He was no longer able to make sense of the sensations that bounced around his brain. Perhaps that's what it means to forget. Everything becomes a whirl of words and colours without any meaning. And there are many ways to forget. Alzheimer's is only one. Drinking and using is another, and the outcome is always the same. You get lost in a Fury of Sensation. You dance in the Chaos until it overwhelms you. Then you cry. Then nothing. Absolutely nothing.

I cooked him breakfast, came home at lunchtime to check on him, and spent all my evenings with him until, one afternoon, I came home and found him in the garden. There was a smell of gas. He had turned the cooker on and gone out to enjoy the afternoon sun. I hadn't a clue what to do except to give him more of myself, and we persevered together for another few weeks. I came home more often during the day and took days off to be with him. Then he left the gas on a second and a third time. I clung on without hope until whatever it was holding us together snapped and I told him:

—Granddad, you're going to a lovely home a short distance away where there's some cracking-looking nurses, so if you play your cards right, you never know.

Nothing. Not even a smile. Then:

—Had some artist mates come round yesterday. Salvador Dalí was one of them. We sat for hours painting the garden fence. Don't know who the rest of them were. Think one of them was bald. Not sure what happened to the paintings after they left. Have you seen them? Might be worth some money.

I visited him most days in the home. It was a decent place but he was out of context and he was dead within a month. The last time I saw him, I thought he didn't recognise me, until he pulled his head out of whatever mincer it was in and said:

—Never forget who you are.

But that's exactly what I do. I forget who I am. People pay to watch me sniff and snort and shag until I pass out before their eyes and I become what they see. I play a part and I've played it so well, I *am* it. I'm a freak show, a circus act that makes the admission fee worth paying. You want a high-wire act, that's me. A clown? That's me, too. The audience, on the other hand, always watches from a safe distance, immunised against what they see. If the wire-walker falls, they gasp and pretend to cover their eyes, but they will be looking, waiting, hoping, because they paid the admission fee to see someone fall. When they tell and re-tell the story of that fall, they will exaggerate it each time, because *they* become more in the telling. First:

—It was awful.

Then:

—I couldn't look. All the broken bones and screams.

Then:

—It was the worst thing imaginable, to watch a man fall and break like glass on the ground. There was blood every-where.

So if I tell my audience I drink a gallon of whisky every morning before having senseless sex with a thousand Wraps and a smattering of Grannies, they will say:

—That's Lincoln!

But if I tell them I am an Artist and I've painted over a hundred canvasses they will say:

—That's not Lincoln!

And although I could take them to see every one of those paintings, they are right. That's not Lincoln because Lincoln forgets. He forgets who he is. He forgets to be kind. He forgets to love. He forgets to create. He forgets everything that matters because he has become a spectacle, and his act is to destroy anything and anyone who stands between him and his Hunger.

As I finish the painting, Esurio walks in. He looks at the canvas.

—Ah, *A Stag at Sharkey's*. A fine painting and a *very* fine copy.

—Thank you.

—It's also reassuring to see that you are connecting with an underworld, Lincoln. I was fearful I might find you copying Monet's *Women in the Garden* but to see fists and fighting and dimly lit basements makes my heart sing.

—It's not the fighting. You know that, don't you? It's not the fighting.

—What do you mean 'it's not the fighting'?

—The fighting isn't why I like it. It's the people-watching, waiting for one of the fighters to get hurt. Really hurt. Even if they lose their bet, the hurt makes it all worthwhile. They make me sick. *You* make me sick.

—I see we've been ruminating again. Does you no good, Lincoln. Here ...

Esurio passes me a glass and pours some red wine into it.

—A very fine vintage. Cheers!

I dare not move my hand. I need this drink. I need it now. I look up at the painting. There is nothing there. The canvas, the paints, the brushes, they're all gone. In their place, Esurio is leering at me:

—Feed me, Lincoln, feed me.

I squeeze the glass so hard I think it will shatter. Again:

—You *must* feed me, Lincoln, you *must*!

—Fuck you!

And that is my battle cry. It is not a cry of attack or victory. It is a cry of resignation. The First Day is for Art and what kind of artist would I be if I was a sober one? I raise the glass to my lips and drink.

—Drink, Lincoln, drink. This is your true self. Accept it, surrender, and take all the pleasure it wants to give you.

He pours me another. And another. He keeps pouring but however many glasses I have, the bottle never seems to empty. I say:

—What sort of bottle is that?

—A special one. I keep it for occasions such as this. Enjoy!

He hands me the bottle. I take it with me when I leave the flat and it stays with me until I'm too drunk to remember where I've left it. I show it to the boys in The Office. They are impressed until they forget about it and say:

—We were worried about you. We hadn't seen you all day. We thought you'd forgotten about us.

—Well, I'm here now and let's get the needle in red!

They cheer. Red means turbo and I go into turbo like no one else. I am, after all, a consummate performer. There comes a point where red turns to black but I do not know when that happens. Black doesn't mean anything cools or slows. It's the point when I pass out, when something turns to nothing, when forgetfulness takes over and the spectacle consumes me.

The Second Day

When I wake up, *A Stag at Sharkey's* is torn to pieces. Bits of bodies are strewn across the room. Paints and brushes litter the floor. There is a Wrap in my bed. I look again. Two Wraps. Coke and booze are everywhere. I don't know whether I created this mess or just walked into it. I grab a quick shower and go for a run. As I pound the streets, leaving Soho in the direction of Knightsbridge, some things are as they always are:

- My head hurts
- My chest hurts
- I am angry
- I need a drink
- I am killing myself

One thing is different. It is a New Thought. Here it is:

Perhaps I should try Abstinence for the next six days. Just to see where it takes me.

I have no idea where this New Thought comes from because I can't think of a single reason why I should abstain from anything. I ask myself a question: If I stop drinking and using, who will I really be? I can barely make sense of the question and any attempt at an answer would be ridiculous. But the New Thought is there and it is Real.

Esurio is nowhere to be seen. I know he'll be unhappy at this change in the way I'm thinking, and he won't be happy until my head is as empty of good ideas as it usually is.

When I get back to the flat, Maynard calls and reminds me we're meeting for lunch. I had forgotten everything about it and, besides, we never make appointments. I'm confused so I ask him:

—Anything in particular?

—Just carrying on from last night.

I haven't a clue what he's talking about. He reads my hesitation.

—Don't worry, I didn't expect you to remember.

—Thank fuck for that.

We meet at The Office. Almost everything is the same as it always is. The wine, the food, the bar. *Almost* everything. After the usual recap of yesterday's madness, the normal frantic anticipation of what might happen today is gone. Maynard looks surprisingly dapper in a blue suit. It's not usual for me to see beyond the gaunt face and the sweat. But today I do. I can't think what it is about him other than he seems like the man he might have been. Our conversation is drifting into familiar dead-ends when he breaks the flow:

—It's what you said last night, Linc. It stuck with me.

—C'mon, man, I have no idea what I said last night. I can't even remember what I *did* last night.

—OK, fair enough. You kept on saying, 'It's over, it's over, it's over . . .'

This is where the Big Story begins. I think the Geek with Glasses said somewhere in the book that Big Stories were a good way of learning. Maynard begins his Big Story placing two fingers parallel to each other on the table.

—Think of these fingers like lines and, when they're like this, however far they stretch into the future they will always be the same distance apart, so nothing really changes. But now imagine I move the left finger just one millimetre to the left. You probably can't even see the difference, but as the lines stretch on and on, a millimetre becomes a centimetre, then a metre, than a kilometre, until a distance opens up between the two lines that's so big you can't even measure it. That's what a small, insignificant change can do. Make it now and your whole life will change because of it.

I have six days left to change my life, so I think the Big Story is a good one, although I don't know what to do with it. Maynard can see this so he hands me a crumpled bit of paper with the address of a chapter of Alcoholics Anonymous in Soho. I am disappointed. He reads my expression like a book:

—I thought you might think that. Not enough for you is it, Linc?

—I suppose not.

—Sorry to disappoint; it's all I have to give. Just give it a go.

—Thanks, Maynard. You're better than all of them.

—No I'm not. I'm one of them and so are you.

Esurio is furious:

—So, Lincoln, you listen to your mate who's some American screenwriter whose best years were never that great and he passes you a box of the toughest tissues, tells you a flimsy fairy tale about a couple of parallel lines and you cry like a baby and decide to quit on me. I thought you were more of a man than that. If I'd have known this side of you, I'd have booked you tickets to see *The Sound of Music* so you could get it out of your system without any real damage being done.

—I haven't quit on you. I never quit. I'm just going to one meeting tonight at seven and you can say what you like, but I owe that to Maynard.

—You owe him nothing, Lincoln, nothing.

—OK, then I owe him nothing but I owe it to myself. I said seven days and I'm doing seven days. Esurio grabs me by the shoulder. I go to grab his throat but before I can get to him he's already a few yards behind me.

—Don't think you can touch me, Lincoln. You can talk all you want about owing and changing but there's one thing you and I know and that is we're joined at the hip like Siamese twins, and there's no getting away from that. Not now. Not ever. So go to your meeting but remember that every path you take leads straight back to me.

The Third Day

I haven't had a drink. No coke either. I think:

—This is easy. I'm probably one of those guys who doesn't really need to go to AA meetings.

Esurio says:

—I don't think you need to go either, so why bother?

When I walk into the room there are maybe a couple of dozen people sitting in a rough semi-circle. I smile at a few of them. They smile back. I wonder what I'm doing here. I'm embarrassed. I want to be in The Office. I decide I'm not going to say anything in the meeting. I take the people in. Most of them are men. Average age, over forty. There are leaflets and books on a table in the corner. On my way in I pick up a copy of *The Big Book* and I bury my head in the Twelve Steps. I convince myself I'm learning. The truth is I'm hiding. My stomach begins twisting. I clench my teeth. I want to hurt someone. Then a man in his sixties starts the meeting by saying something about a 'fellowship' and he reads a prayer. I sit and listen and think about The Office until a young man says:

—Hi, I'm Jason and I'm an alcoholic.

The group responds:

—Hi Jason.

He goes on:

—I want to thank everyone here for helping me on the road to recovery. When I first came I found the Steps hard, almost impossible. I was ashamed of what I had done to those closest to me and frightened because I didn't believe in a Higher Power or God or anything like that; there was nothing or no one to restore me to sanity. Bill, my sponsor, said, 'Just think of it as something that's more important than you. A parent, a child, a book you're writing, nature, anything.' I did and I dedicated it to my son. I hadn't seen him for four years because my ex-wife thought I was a danger to him and blocked access. Well, he's four and a half now and this week I saw him for the first time since he was a baby.

Some of the group applaud. Others wipe away a tear. A few seem unmoved. And so it goes on. People stand and talk; it's called 'sharing', and they talk about acceptance and humility and powerlessness and God.

I feel sick.

I want a drink.

I don't believe in God.

I wonder if going to the meeting was such a good idea.

I think about my son, Lewis. He's eighteen now.

I last saw him a month ago. We met at seven o'clock in the Townhouse. I was sober. When I know Lewis is coming to see me I stay as clean as I can. We hugged each other as we always do and I felt his anger. And his love. We sat in silence opposite each other at a table near the bar. Then he said:

—You know I can see it, don't you?

—What?

—What you're doing to yourself.

I didn't respond, and we spent the next hour talking about this and that as shame washed over me in waves. As soon as he left I drank a bottle of Grand Cru and put as much coke up my nose as my nostrils could take. The worst feeling a man can have is to feel less than his son, to be a father in name only. It's as if someone has given me a label and said, 'That's who you are now, a father', but however much I read the label I can't connect it to the person I feel I am. It's not that I feel I don't deserve my son's love. It's deeper than that. I don't even deserve to *give* love, let alone receive it. If 'father' is a feeling then how can I be a father, when I'm a screaming, helpless, terrified child, too busy trying to scrape my own Dad's dead body off the ground at a caravan park to grow up and be a father in my own right? I have never been fully formed; it's like I got stuck in that moment and all I have ever done is bang my head against the bars of that cage, waiting for them to break from the pressure, but they never do.

My mother or my ex-wife, perhaps both of them, said:

—Lewis idolises you.

Lewis said:

—I just want to be like you. You're a hero to me.

When he said this, I thought:

—I like being idolised by my son.

Then I thought:

Life is easier when people look down on you, when they have no expectations and you're free to be the total cunt they believe you to be.

I said to my Mum:

—I would die for Lewis but his love is killing me.

In the meeting, I find myself standing on my feet. I say:

—Hi, I'm Lincoln. I'm an alcoholic and I'm powerless over my drinking and I want to dedicate my recovery to my father and to my son, Lewis.

When I look up I see Esurio shaking his head in the corner of the room. He takes off his hat and does an extravagant bow:

—Bravo, Lincoln, bravo!

I want to kill him. I want to leap over the chairs and ring his fucking neck. Before I can move, he has gone. On the way out, he is waiting for me by the door.

—Quite a performance in there. Reminded me of a church. It doesn't seem like you at all, Lincoln, and I fear it will finish you off if you start believing.

—Give it a rest. If I want to be there, I'll be there. It's only for a week.

He pulls a crumpled bit of paper out of his pocket.

—OK then, let's look at some of these grand steps. Here. The first one: *We admitted we were powerless over alcohol, that our lives had become unmanageable.* That's hardly you, is it?

—What do you mean?

—Well, you are many things, Lincoln, but powerless isn't one of them. You consume whatever you want, when you want. That, if you ask me, is the action of a strong, confident man – a man who knows what he wants and takes it.

—That's fair enough, I suppose.

—And how about this one: *We admitted to God, to ourselves and to another human being the exact nature of our wrongs.* When was the last time you brought God into anything and, let's be candid, you have certainly not done anything *wrong*. A little misguided at times, perhaps, even a touch over the top, but *wrong*? 'Wrong' is an unkind word, Lincoln, very unkind. It's a word designed to break a man, to take away his dignity, and I have certainly not gone to all the trouble of teaching you how to dress, of watching you blossom into a man dedicated only to joy and pleasure, for someone to call it 'wrong'. And what kind of person, Lincoln, what kind of person uses a word like 'wrong'?

I don't want to hear him but, one by one, his words, like relentless drops of water washing up against a crumbling wall, are finding a way through.

—I don't know, I don't know, I don't *want* to know.

—Ah, you see, there it is. The Admission of Wilful Ignorance. Well, let me tell you about the person who uses a word like 'wrong'. It is a weak person, like the fearful hordes who fill places of worship, who use all their energy to judge the few, the mighty few, for whom a word like 'wrong' does not exist.

We stop outside the Soho Theatre on Dean Street.

—And that you don't *want* to know, Lincoln, shows how just one meeting has weakened you. I fear if you continue going I will not recognise you, my own brother, my twin, and we will become strangers to each other.

—Please leave me alone. Please.

—I'm afraid I can't do that, Lincoln. What kind of friend would I be if I let you hurt yourself in this way? Life is to be lived and they will have you cowering in a corner in no time at all. What kind of man do you want to be? One whom the ladies adore, who sweeps all before him, who rises above his own excesses and lives a life free from fear, or a little mouse afraid of his own shadow?

Esurio furrows his brow, lowers his head, brings his hands under his chin and squeaks.

—And the worse thing they will do is make you believe that you are ordinary when you, Lincoln, are a man apart from the rest. You can drink more, snort more, sniff more, run more, exercise more and pleasure more ladies than any man in Soho, and while doing all this you can still not only hold down a job but earn the right to be the highest-paid Sales Director of a gentlemen's club in London. So tell me, exactly how are you powerless? What are you doing wrong? What faults do you have to admit to? Face the truth, Lincoln, Alcoholics Anonymous is not for you. It may serve a purpose but for you it can only do harm, great harm. It will make you look back at what you have lost in life, make your strengths into weaknesses, your courage into wrongdoing. It will make you give up on yourself when you are at the peak of your powers and it will take away from you all that you value most in life and everything that brings you happiness. Stop it now. NOW!

I turn into Old Compton Street, open the door to my flat and slam it in his face. I'm asleep as soon as I hit my bed. My sleep is fitful and I am drunk in my dreams.

Truth and Other Lies

The Fourth Day

Recovery is strange because I never thought I was lost and I have no idea what kind of man will appear from the wreckage, assuming I can get to him before the seven days are up.

Esurio says:

—Lost? Far from it, Lincoln. You are absolutely in touch with your essence but I'm so concerned that you're in danger of forgetting who you are and what makes you happy. I fear you've already forgotten your one, true friend.

Being sober is like peeling away a thick layer of skin. It doesn't fall away all at once. Bits of it break off here and there and, as they do, I notice things. This morning I was running along the Embankment and my head was clear. I thought about new ways to leverage relationships with the concierges to bring more punters into The Club. I thought about doing a *Jet Set* in the South of France and I called my Mum to tell her I would come round to build her a small rock pool in the back garden. She said:

—That's lovely, darling.

Then:

—Are you all right?

That's the thing about clarity in drunks. It shocks people. They get used to your hazy, virtual life, then you mess up their world with a shocking display of sobriety. Some people want you to stay clean. Most can't take it and fear they might get contaminated. These are the people who touch me all over, looking for the skin we used to share and, when they can't find it, they think:

—He's lost his skin! Does that mean I will lose mine too? But I don't *want* to lose it. I'm not ready to lose it, and I don't want to be around him until he grows it back.

When I go into The Office, the boys are split. After a week of drinking water and chamomile tea, Maynard and I are having lunch at our usual table near the bar. He says:

—You're doing well. I'm really pleased for you.

The others treat me like a freak. Terry says:

—So, you're not drinking anything?

—No. Not unless you count tea and water as a drink.

—I fucking don't. Surely you can have one?

—I don't want one.

—Not even one for old times' sake?

—One is never one. One might as well be a hundred and one.

—You sound like a psychology textbook.

—I just don't want a drink.

Steve joins in:

—Does that mean you've stopped shagging as well?

—Of course not.

—Thank fuck for that. At least a little bit of the Old Lincoln is still with us.

The Old Lincoln

But which bit? Here's what I notice when I'm fucking Wraps while sober:

- I pound for hours just like I always did.
- I find this reassuring.
- In fact, I do my best to break more beds than ever.
- I find this reassuring too.
- Wraps and broken beds are less important to me than they were before.
- I find this worrying.
- I sometimes feel I can't be bothered with Wraps.
- I find this even more worrying.
- When I feel this I go out of my way to fuck two or three of them at a time.
- For old times' sake.
- I find myself *connecting* with them.
- I know this because I feel grateful.
- I think I have feelings for some of them.
- I like talking to them.
- I cry with some of them.
- They massage me and tell me they love me.
- I want to hold them in my hand and keep them safe from harm.
- I take some of them away from Soho.
- *Away from Soho!*
- We go walking in the Lake District or we go to Southend for a day by the sea or we visit my Mum.
- I notice I am using Paid-Fors less often than I used to.

- One day I think:

There's not much left of the Old Lincoln.

- This thought frightens me, so I hire four Paid-Fors and we go to the Sanderson Hotel.
- I bang them but it doesn't *feel* like it used to.
- I wonder if I should have a drink to get that feeling back. Esurio says:

—Have one, Lincoln, have one. Just one.

- I consider it, then I think:

Maybe the Old Lincoln wasn't that great.

- I spend a few minutes thinking about the difference between the Old and New Lincoln.
- I make a list of the bits of the Old Lincoln that are still with me. I can think only of:
  - Vanity
  - Anger
  - Pounding
  - I think about what I like most about the New Lincoln. I write:
  - Clarity

Because I like having a clear head, I decide to stick with the New Lincoln, so I say to Steve:

—Yeah, the Old Lincoln's still with us. He's just nicer.

I decide to keep going to the meetings. They tell me the best way to do it is to go for ninety meetings in ninety days. I wonder how many I can get to in the ninety hours I have left to change my life. I'm indifferent to what happens in the meetings. When I'm there I drift in and out. No one intrudes and no one touches me, which is great. I sometimes speak to people at meetings. They tell me stories. I don't like these conversations. I want to get away. I want a drink and a line. I look at my watch often, counting the minutes away. Some of the people in the group don't speak. Others fill the time with Tales of Misery and Despair. I find these Tales reassuring. They are like fairy tales that teach me that my life at its worst doesn't seem too bad by comparison: *Once upon a time there was a man who lived all his life on the streets. His wife left him. His kids disowned him. So he drank and drank and drank until he couldn't drink anymore and that's when he slashed his wrists with a broken beer bottle. When he was discharged from hospital he went back on the streets and drank all night and cried all day. Lincoln, on the other hand, was having a Great Time banging all the Wraps in Soho and snorting coke off their arses . . .*

By the end of the second meeting I'm pretty sure I don't have a drink problem and if I do it's as mild as a common cold, while the rest of the poor fuckers in the meeting have a serious dose of the plague. However, I am changing my life, so I will stick to Abstinence until the end of the week and I'm surprised at how good I feel. After one of the meetings, I share a bottle of water on the top floor of Soho House with John, who has been in recovery for two years. I never liked Soho House. Too full of pissed-up actors. We sit on a couple of battered leather chairs. The place is heaving. Someone bumps into me as I walk across the creaking floorboards. Someone else touches my glass before I can pick it up off the bar. I want to kill them both but the feeling passes. *It passes. Without any broken bones or bleeding noses.* I like John. He is in his mid-forties, dressed in jeans and a casual brown jacket. I admire his indifference to how he looks. He used to work as an A&R man at a big record label before he lost his job for turning up pissed to work once too often. I say:

—I thought being pissed was part of your employment contract in that industry.

—It is. But what you mustn't do is be so pissed you forget your place.

I don't ask what happened. I don't need to. When he cleaned himself up, he began working at an art gallery.

—I don't really enjoy it. Looking all day at conceptual crap that could have been done by failed art college students.

—Why work there then?

—Because it takes absolutely nothing out of me. Nothing.

—Don't you want to be more challenged?

—That's the last thing I want. I need every ounce of energy I have to keep me dry, so having a job that takes nothing out of me is just what I need.

—What happens when you get bored?

—It happens all the time and I love being bored at work. Gives me time to think, prepare for a meeting if I'm leading it. I don't know, just lots of space, lots and lots of space, that's what I need.

—Surely you can't go on forever like this? There has to come a time when you want more.

—Forever? Most days I can't look forward twenty-four hours. Recovery isn't something I can bolt on to my life. It *is* my life. It has to be. If I had cancer or motor neurone disease or I was paralysed from a stroke, I would put everything I have into my recovery. Drinking like I do is a terminal illness. If I forget that I'm fucked. So what more do I need in my life than getting through another day without killing myself?

I leave Soho House just after ten to go to The Club. As I walk down Old Compton Street I can smell aniseed. I turn and Esurio is walking with me:

—Well, he was a barrel of laughs, wasn't he, Lincoln?

—Give it a fucking rest.

—I'm not trying to be difficult but sometimes I feel compelled to speak truthfully.

—Truthfully?

—Yes, truthfully. If there's one thing you can rely on me for, it's honesty, and I have to say the more of these people I see, the more I'm certain they're not good for you, Lincoln, not good for you at all.

—These people?

—These ... Believers ... Evangelists ... the Devoutly Wretched.

—Give them a break. They're just struggling.

—And so, may I remind you, was every martyr who ever walked the face of the earth before leaving it in a blaze of stupidity.

—What are you talking about?

—Life is for living, Lincoln, not for dying, and these new friends of yours may be walking and breathing but they are dead. They died the day they gave over their lives to one small, sneaky, dirty little word.

—And what word is that then?

—NO. The worst word ever created.

He keeps on at me until we get to The Club but I stop listening to him. When I leave him, he is standing in the drizzle outside The Club going on about the Truth. Inside there's not many punters. They tend to turn up from about midnight onwards. Two guys in front of me walk into The Club.

They're pounced on by Wraps. It's White Lingerie Night, and they disappear into a snowstorm of barely covered tits and pussy. I don't like it, it's too much, so when the guys are trapped in a booth with a couple of Russian Wraps, I let a few of the girls know what I think:

—Always give the guys time. If you keep doing that they'll all fuck off and then you won't earn anything.

They ignore me. I don't like being ignored. I need a drink. The Boss is sitting on his throne in his restaurant. He calls me over.

—I'm proud of you, Lincoln.

—What for?

—Giving up the booze.

—Thanks.

I forget I need a drink. The Boss matters to me. There's not a lot of people that do, but he's one of them. He gets up and puts his arm around my shoulder. He's wearing a turquoise suit with *Ziggy Stardust* written down the outside of one trouser leg. The glitter in his hair and on his clothes glistens in the roller-ball lights. All the Wraps look at him. He ignores them. He leans into my ear:

—Don't let this go. It's the right thing for you to be doing. I never want to see you hammered in here again. Who's coming tonight?

—I've got more bankers than usual and a lot of punters, sorry, *Gentlemen*, coming from the hotels. I've been sending three girls out every day to get at the concierges.

Sometimes I hope I'm right. Usually I'm too pissed to care whether I'm right. Tonight I know I'm right. That's what being sober does for me. Instead of thinking I'm the best Sales Director in the universe, I know I'm the best Sales Director in Soho because I'm sober. The Boss's mantra bounces around my head:

—Keep it real, Lincoln, keep it real.

Rik and his gang turn up at about one in the morning. I haven't seen him since he was banging a Wrap in my bed. He offers to buy me a drink. I tell him I'm not drinking. I think he doesn't hear me because he offers again. I tell him I'm not drinking. He *can't* hear me, so he buys me a drink anyway. I sit him at one of the best tables downstairs, right in front of the stage, and order two bottles of house champagne on my account. I sit with him for a few minutes. He pours me three glasses. I don't drink any of them. When I get up to leave they're still standing in a row on the table. He *can't* see them. He asks me if I enjoyed them, tells me he's glad I'm drinking again and gets back to the Wraps.

The night goes well. It was the most profitable White Lingerie Night The Club has ever run. The following morning I walk into The Office. I do not lean on the door. I am not sweating. I spend a few minutes running through the numbers with Mark. The Boss calls me into his office. I've prepared a schedule of parties for him running until the summer.

—I've put two parties for the concierges, four parties for the bankers, a Poker Night and maybe we could introduce some new themed nights like this one.

I've prepared a flyer for a party I've called *Heels and Wheels*, showing a couple of topless Wraps spread all over a Porsche 911.

—I thought we could go to Porsche or Ferrari and get them to park a car outside The Club and inside we can theme it like the sexiest car showroom in the world. I might even talk to McLaren and see if we can get a Formula 1 car in The Club.

—What other parties can we hold?

—How about a *Dinners for Sinners* party and we can get Marco in to do the food? There's loads, but what I want to do is hammer the Diamond Card Holders. We've got maybe four thousand of them on the database and we don't work them like we should. They've got the card because they spend the money. They buy the Cristal champagne, they get a dozen girls in for sit-downs, so I've thought about a special club just for Big Spenders. I've called it the *Secret Society*. It's a step on from the *Jet Set*. They pay maybe ten large each to join and we hold parties for them in The Club but also in villas in Cannes, Palma or the Algarve. We'll fly the girls out and maybe twenty society members will pay an extra ten grand each for the weekend.

The Boss is looking at me as if he's meeting me for the first time.

The Fifth Day

The next day The Boss calls in before he flies to Ibiza. He puts a contract in front of me.

—Stay sober and I'll double your money. Drink and I'll halve it.

I sign it. Five days and my life is already changing. What will it be like after seven?

It feels too good to be sober. I have started doing two hours instead of one every day in the gym. I'm bench-pressing over a hundred kilograms and doing over three hundred press-ups.

I run at least five miles a day and there are even days when I don't have sex. I'm shocked by my own thoughts. When I was running across the Heath before going into work, this is what came into my head:

I must read some books on psychology.

I'll pay Bruno the money I owe him this afternoon. I'll throw in a bottle of champagne as a thank you.

Who would I really be if I never drank again?

I want to give Suzie a grand. She's struggling with her rent. I don't want the money back.

The sun feels good on my back.

I feel happy.

Ecstatic.

I love The Boss.

I owe him more than he ever knows.

Who would I really be if I never drank again?

I must call my Mum and go round to build her that rock pool.

I never knew being sober was this easy.

I'll keep going to the meetings even though I don't really need them anymore.

I've lost the taste for alcohol.

I'd rather have coffee than cocaine.

The Secret Society is a brilliant idea.

Esurio's right. People like John make heavy weather of staying dry.

I can be sober and happy.

I meet Suzie. After we fuck I give her the rent money. She hugs me and says:

—One day I'll marry you, Lincoln. It might be five or ten years from now but I will.

I am thirty-eight. She's nineteen. Her mother kicked her

out of the house when she was a teenager and she went to live in a caravan on the south coast. She says:

—I just want a family. With you.

We fuck again.

I go to a meeting in the evening. During a break I say to John:

—Two days to go.

He looks at me. Like he is meeting me for the first time. And the last.

When I leave the meeting, I'm walking along Shaftesbury Avenue when I think:

—After the seven days are up I'll keep going to the meetings. It'll just be occasional. Maybe once or twice a month. I don't need them but Tales of Misery and Despair are good for my soul.

I catch my reflection in the glass of the Curzon Cinema and adjust my handkerchief.

In the afternoon before the meeting I went to dig the rock pool at my Mum's house. I was relentless. The early spring sunshine was beating down on me and I pounded the earth for maybe two or three hours without stopping. As I was beating the ground I smiled at how, even now, without a drop of alcohol or a grain of gear in my body, I still couldn't stop. It took me three hours. Mum said:

—Thank you, darling. That's lovely.

Then:

—You're a good lad, Lincoln. Underneath it all, you're a very good lad.

But underneath what? And how far does she have to dig to find a seam of decency?

We never had any money when I was growing up, and after Dad died things got even worse. So I used to go to school and boast about how rich we were, how we could afford anything we wanted. My Mum said:

—It's no use lying all the time. It doesn't change anything.

She was wrong. It changed everything. I learned that if my world was breaking apart, I had the power to put it back together again in any way I wanted. This is how the process works:

Their Lie: We haven't got any money.
My Truth: We can afford anything we want.
Their Lie: You'll get caught.
My Truth: I'll always get away with it.
Their Lie: My Mum can see through me like glass.
My Truth: I can hide anything from anyone.
Their Lie: If you carry on drinking and using, you'll
            have a heart attack like your Dad.
My Truth: I'm going to live forever.
Their Lie: You're in pain.
My Truth: I love pleasure.

And there was another reason I didn't have to lie. We were, in fact, rich in ways I couldn't see, as my gaze was lost in the search for the money we never had. Here's the evidence I missed as I struggled to solve *The Mystery of the Missing Money*:

- My Dad took me dog-racing at Dalston and we ate pies and jellied eels.
- My parents never argued.
- They laughed together. A lot.

- Dad took me to the seaside and we ran down a long pier and played on the fruit machines.
- My Dad knew Marty Wilde and we all played golf together.
- My parents took me to the Tower of London and didn't leave me there.
- My Dad had a great sense of humour.
- He made me laugh. A lot.

But when you're a wounded detective and you can't stop trying to solve *The Mystery of the Missing Money*, you can't see the truth because you're too busy laying down one false trail after another and following them all as fast as you can, in the hope that one day you can find a reason to stop running.

The Sixth Day

Being sober feels like a drug.

I'm in a meeting and, as I look around the room, I feel sorry for the people who have been coming to these meetings for years, so at the end of the meeting I stand up and say:

—I want to thank everyone here and those who aren't here today for helping me stop drinking. I couldn't have done it without you.

I feel a bit of a toady because the truth is I know I could have done it without them but this is the New, Nicer Lincoln. I like him and so do they. I tell them that Esurio has a special party organised for me on The Seventh Day, so I won't be at tomorrow's meeting but, before I sit down again, I add:

—You've helped me rediscover my True Self. Thank you.

I don't know where that came from, but when I'm walking along Wardour Street after the meeting Esurio is chuckling at my shoulder.

—Ah, your True Self. That was a bit grand, don't you think?

—Maybe, but it's true.

He is swinging his cane as he walks. He's brighter than I've seen him for some time. He sneers at me:

—What, Lincoln, is Truth?

—Don't get all clever with me. I'm just saying, being sober feels like being me.

—Oh, dear, you really are in a muddle.

—What do you mean?

—If there is such a thing as a True Self, I imagine yours to be . . . mud-coloured

—Mud-coloured?

—Let me put it another way. How can you be sure that the man walking along this street with me right now, taking in the lights and ladies at a safe distance, is the real you? Are you not a murkier man than that, Lincoln?

—Less murky than I was.

—I see. So when did this great change take place?

—I don't know. It just happened on the Fifth Day.

—I grant you that a change has taken place in you, but how can you be sure that this change isn't taking you *away* from your True Self, as you like to call him?

I wipe the back of my right hand across my lips. I can hear Esurio laughing. When I turn to smack him, he is nowhere to be seen.

After the meeting, I'm pleased with myself. I think:

—Quite an achievement. At least now I can get on with my life.

I crease my brow.

—But which life am I going to get on with?

I don't like that question, so I ignore it, although I can't shift it completely out of my head. Danielle comes into my mind. She was a Wrap who worked in Soho. She started as a dancer and ended up as a Paid-For. Then she fell in love with a punter. They were married within three months and before the wedding all she could talk about was what she would be wearing, how her little nieces were going to be bridesmaids and how she wanted a 'chocolate box' wedding. The Big Day was her wall, too thick and tall for her to see past it, so she got married. The beatings started on her honeymoon and within a month she was back in Soho. Three weeks later she was dead. As I leave the meeting, I think:

—This is my Big Day. I made it.

When I come out of the meeting, I find myself standing outside The Office. I can't remember walking there. One minute I'm in the meeting. The next I'm outside The Office. I can see the boys at the back, laughing. A few Wraps are hanging around, waiting for some coke and taking cock as payment. Esurio puts his hand on my shoulder.

—Go in, Lincoln. You haven't been in for quite a while, have you?

I walk towards Oxford Street. I feel Doubt. Not about anything in particular, just a gnawing, mud-coloured Doubt twisting in my gut. Seven Days? Is it enough? Does the Geek with Glasses really know what he's talking about?

On the night of The Sixth Day I go to bed early and dream of snorting some gear off a Wrap's back. As my head touches her skin, her spine, in the form of a snake, breaks out of her body and twists around my throat. I wake up gasping for breath. Then I'm in The Office and I order a vodka tonic. I'm alone at the table when Mario brings it to me. He serves it to me as if he's been expecting me for some time. He seems pleased I'm back. I look at it forever. I can feel the smell rising up into my nostrils and circulating through my body. I inhale deeply and hold my breath. Then I let go. I dare not touch the glass. I know if I touch it I will be lost. I need a drink. I need *this* drink. NOW. I sit there for maybe half an hour then something pulls me out of my seat and within seconds I'm running through Soho. I'm laughing. People stare at me then lower their heads. They think I'm insane. They're right. I'm mad with happiness. I passed the test. I sat there and I didn't drink. I am Immortal. Powerful Beyond Measure. I wake up sweating and smiling. My chest hurts. I ignore it and wipe my hand across my lips.

The Seventh Day

I begin the Seventh Day with a trip to the best Thai massage parlour on Brewer Street. A stunning Asian Wrap bends me like a doll before giving me the happiest of happy endings. When she's done I wonder if I should stop thinking of young women as Wraps. They can be Girls. Simple, beautiful Girls. I walk out of the massage parlour and Esurio is standing on the opposite side of the road. He's smiling.

—It's the Seventh Day, Lincoln, and I want you to see just how much your life has changed. Tonight you will have as many young ladies as you wish without a drop of alcohol passing your lips. I feel you are ready to start a new life where you have more control over your impulses, where you can indulge one pleasure without being overrun by another. Let's meet in the Townhouse on Dean Street and take it from there. Bravo, Lincoln, bravo!

I smile back at him, proud of how far I've come in such a short time. I spend the rest of the day getting myself ready. I go for a facial in Mayfair and, when I get back to the flat, I take a couple of hours removing surplus body hair before going to the gym.

In the evening I am not hungry. I get a sandwich from Starbucks and on my way back I think of how my life has changed over the last Seven Days. A week ago there was me and the drink and the drugs and we were all heading in the same direction. Then I took a small step on a different path and now we are worlds apart. I guess it's what happens when parallel lives go their separate ways. That is the Truth. My Truth. How difficult can that be to grasp?

The Grand Ball of
Immortal Addicts

Midnight on The Seventh Day

I'm sitting by the bar in the Townhouse.
    I'm drinking a glass of water.
    I'm sober.
    I wipe my hand across my mouth.
    I look at my watch. Esurio will be here any minute.

9 p.m. on The Seventh Day

I'm in my flat on Old Compton Street with two Regulars, an
Occasional and a Paid-For.
    I am bored.
    No amount of anal can raise my spirits.
    After an hour I put a hundred and fifty on the bedside table
for the Paid-For and leave the Wraps to get on with it.
    As I walk down the stairs I have this thought:
    —When you have changed your life, what happens next?

10:15 p.m. on The Seventh Day

I bump into Lisa, the Pilates teacher on Berwick Street. She's in her early seventies and one of the sexiest women I know. I banged her once a few months ago. I think if I bang her again it might raise my spirits.

—Lincoln, this is Joanna. She's one of my Pilates students.

Joanna is a petite, little Wrap with one of those pretty, picture-book faces. I imagine what that face would look like after I fuck her. I smile at her and shake her hand with just enough pressure for her to know what I want. She smiles. Nervously. She waits for me to let her hand go. The deal is done: passive Wraps are easily banged. I say:

—Let's go for a drink.

Lisa replies:

—Sure. Where do you fancy?

—Well, I'm off the booze and the gear at the moment, so it's up to you.

Lisa looks at me like I have beamed down from a distant galaxy.

—Well ... that's ... great ... great ... Are you sure you have ... I mean ...

—I've changed my life in seven days.

She looks relieved. I don't understand her relief but I seem familiar to her again.

—That's OK then. Why don't we get a coffee at my flat? We were going there anyway.

Joanna follows close behind us, her hand touching my arm when she speaks.

Lisa's flat is littered with pictures of the Buddha and some old prints of Asians banging. It stinks of incense.

She puts on some music. I look at the CD cover: half-a-dozen Wraps dressed like angels and chanting to some pipes. I imagine banging them until I realise they bore me. I look at Joanna. She says something about the fucking universe and waves her arms above her head in a soft, rhythmic movement. I think she really needs a good pounding to sort her head out. I'm just about to surrender and leave when I have a thought:

I've never banged a Granny and a Wrap at the same time.

I have another thought:

My life can never be complete until I bang a Granny and a Wrap at the same time.

I say to Joanna:

—That's lovely the way you move your hands above your head. Shall we all do it together?

—That's a wonderful idea! Why don't we do a sacred circle?

In a few minutes, we're all hugging, touching, waving, while that ridiculous fucking music drones on in the background. This is what happens next:

I kiss Joanna.

She likes it.

Lisa freaks out.

She says: Lincoln! She's my student. Not with her . . .

I begin taking Joanna's clothes off.

Lisa gets up to leave.

She says: Lincoln! I've never done it with one of my students.

We both pull Lisa towards us.

Gently.

She looks at me.

Joanna strokes her.

Gently.

I say: Why don't you connect to Joanna's energy?

They begin to touch and then the first kiss.

I think: I am a fucking genius.

They strip. The Wrap is nice but Lisa is *compelling*.

She may be a Pilates teacher, but she is still a Granny in her seventies and it shows. I love the maturity in her face. The flow of her body. And the sadness she hides in her crystals and bells.

I look at them, a Granny and a Wrap. My Spiritual Bitches.

They fuse into one body

I don't like being left out.

I look for a way in.

Every road is blocked.

I wish I had some gear.

But I don't have any gear and, without it, the coiled fury doesn't spring into life.

I take a last look at them.

They are *serene*.

Their world is not mine.

I think: I want to destroy their world.

Then I think: I want to belong to their world.

I feel pain.

I wonder who the pain belongs to.

I lower my head as I leave.

Esurio opens the door for me and says: I hope you're happy with the change, Lincoln.

Just after Midnight on The Seventh Day

I hear Esurio before I see him:

—A bit disappointing earlier, don't you think?

—Back off!

—Oh, please don't misunderstand me. I'm as proud of the way you have changed your life as you are. It just seems like it might have gone a bit too far too soon.

I turn to see him standing beside me, squeezing his thumb and forefinger together to illustrate his point.

—Look, I'm not drinking or using, if that's what you're suggesting. I may have messed up earlier but the pounding is still there. It just takes a little more to get it going.

Steve, the barman, passes me a glass of water:

—You don't look yourself, Lincoln.

Esurio whispers in my ear:

—Everyone can see, Lincoln. Except you.

I bang my fist on the bar.

—See *what* for fuck's sake?

—What you're missing out on. That you're not being the person you're meant to be.

—And who the fuck are you to tell me anything?

—Who am I, Lincoln? After all this time, do you really have to ask?

—Yeah, I do. Who the fuck are you to mess with my life?

—I can show you who I am if you have the courage to look.

—You think I'm frightened? Of looking? At *you*?

Esurio taps his cane on the floor and draws me into his eyes. They are two dark pools, swirling, spinning, and I feel I'm sinking into them. I want to look away but I have no strength. I am cold and helpless, like a child carried off in the night. He waves something across my face. It is too dark to see what it is. I feel nauseous.

—Not feeling well, are we?

I try to reply but I can't move my mouth.

—Best get some air, Lincoln.

I follow him out to the back of the Townhouse. I am behind him as we walk through the bar, but all I can sense is darkness swirling around me. I am struggling for breath. When we're outside I feel the cold air across my face and the sound of his voice ebbs and flows like a giant wave in my head:

—Who am I, Lincoln? Who am I? Who . . .

I cover my ears but the wave gets bigger and louder until it's crashing inside my skull and I pass out.

When I open my eyes I don't feel awake. I hear Esurio tap his cane on the ground again as he passes his gloved hand across my face and I am deep inside the dark pools, lost, without a will of my own.

I have never been at the back of the Townhouse before and, as the darkness breaks in patches, I notice a flight of battered-looking steps leading to a door. There are dustbins on some of them, full of empty bottles, and rats peer at me through the weeds and half-smoked cigarettes. Esurio is sitting on a step, drinking a vintage absinthe.

—If you really want to know who I am, follow me in, Lincoln, follow me in.

I walk up the steps and open the door. Inside the smell is thick and musty. There's a bar with some old photographs behind it and the walls are painted sickly green. There are paintings and drawings everywhere and the till is one of those old ones with buttons and levers. A striking-looking woman in her fifties with dark hair, black gloves and smoking from a long, silver cigarette holder comes over to me. She says:

—Hello, Cunty, are you a member?

I stare at her, unable to move my lips, pushing anger out of my eyes. I think:

—Did she just call me a cunt?

She turns to Esurio:

—She looks very touchy, doesn't she?

—Afraid so. He's just changed his life.

—And why, Dearie, would she want to do that?

I want to tell her to stop calling me 'she' but I have lost the power of speech. The woman carries on talking to Esurio:

—Best get her a seat in the corner. She looks like she might faint.

Esurio pulls an old wooden chair under me, like the ones I used to sit on as a kid in school. Even through the dim light in this room, I can see into the grain of the chair, deeper than I have ever seen into anything. After what feels like hours, Esurio taps his cane on the ground, tells me to sit down and, when I do, the woman asks:

—I forgot to ask. Is she a member? Has she got one of these?

I look up and she's waving a crumpled, brown piece of paper in front of me with some writing on it. The letters have a life of their own. Esurio sorts them out for me:

—It says: Colony Room, 41 Dean Street, W1. Membership Card.

The Colony Room Club. I'm in the fucking Colony Room Club. I look again at the woman and, for the first time, I know who she is: Muriel Belcher. Founder of the Colony Room Club. I remember she is dead and then she continues:

—Tell her not to worry about membership. I know who she is. She's famous in Soho and you know how I adore the Great and the Bad.

She touches my cheek with her gloved fingers and hands me a card. I can just about make out the words *Lifetime Member* before everything goes black and, when I can see again, there are bright lights above the bar and the Colony Room is getting bigger. The green walls are moving away from me so fast I feel sick, until the room is so big I can't see where it ends. I feel soft fabrics rubbing against my hands and, when I look down I'm sitting on a throne covered in jewels and the finest furs. I turn to Esurio and, for the first time, I can speak. The words sputter out of my mouth:

—What's happening to me? Who *are* you?

Esurio leans over to me:

—All in good time, Lincoln.

Muriel is blowing smoke in his hair. He continues:

—I realise you have achieved so much in a short space of time. A mere seven days. But abstinence is not in your nature, Lincoln, so Muriel and I have organised a Grand Ball in memory of your excesses.

Esurio opens his arms and gestures to the vast, empty room:

—Even this room is barely big enough to accommodate all those who come to honour your insatiable appetites. You are a strong man and I have no doubt you will end the night without a drop of alcohol on your lips, but I have become concerned at, how shall I put it, the *seriousness* of your life in recent weeks, so tonight you will live like you have never lived before.

He pounds his cane against the wooden floor:

—Let the Grand Ball of Immortal Addicts begin!

I stare into the vast green room and as far my eye can see there are bar stools, wooden tables, ashtrays, endless bottles of wines and spirits and long, winding trails of white powder stretching along a torn green carpet potholed with cigarette burns. 'Don't Fence Me In', an old Bing Crosby song my Granddad used to listen to, is filling the room with sound and, in the distance, the first guest arrives and walks towards us. He's fat, wearing a dark suit and pink, spotted shirt with a black tie and red trilby. It's George fucking Melly. He nods in my direction and I think:

He's dead, too, like Muriel.

He begins drinking a glass of wine. I notice the bottle he's drinking from never seems to empty and, however many glasses he pours himself, there's always more.

Within minutes the room is full of people smoking, drinking, snorting, shagging, and I am strangely sober. The room has stopped moving, I seem able to speak again and I can see with a clarity and depth I have never experienced before. One after another, the guests come and bow before me. Esurio taps me on the shoulder:

—Go among them. Let them get closer to you.

I step down off the podium. The ballroom is a mass of bodies. They all drink, some snort, others shag and they are all dead. Tallulah Bankhead, Charles Laughton and countless others who lived invisible lives on the streets of Soho. All drunk. All dead. Yet they look so *well*. Everyone is drinking bottle after bottle, taking one line after another, and it makes them stronger, happier, healthier. I turn to Esurio:

—But these people are dead!

—Such talent for excess never dies, Lincoln. It goes on and

on forever. These people can never die. They always want more. They finish ten bottles of the finest wine and they consume another hundred; one rock of the magic white powder and they demand a mountain. They have sat in this room and lived and loved in Soho and you, Lincoln, are one of them and potentially the greatest of them all.

I look to my left and see an impish man surrounded by paints and canvasses. His face has a random, ruddy tint to it, as if he has applied rouge in a haphazard way. He is clearly drunk and often stoops to drink from a bottle of Bollinger on the ground next to his easel. His concentration is so intense he makes me feel that if he doesn't finish what he's doing, the whole world might collapse around him. When he's done, he gets up. He can barely stand but somehow he makes his way towards me, his easel floating alongside him. When he gets to the podium he turns the easel around so I can see what he has been painting. I gasp. It's the 'Screaming Pope' but, instead of Innocent X, he has painted *me* sitting on the papal throne. Esurio smiles down at him:

—Thank you, Francis. Lincoln will be grateful beyond measure.

—My pleasure, Master. To seduce is everything.

I turn to Esurio. I do not understand:

—Why does he call you Master?

—Because my name is Esurio and we are many.

I haven't a fucking clue what he's on about. Esurio senses my confusion:

—To make it simple for you, Lincoln, where you find pain, there you will find me; where you see a man in the gutter, I am with him. Even the greatest artists and the purest minds know me. I am in every glass and every bottle, I dance on the point of every needle and skip on every line. I am everywhere there is Chaos. That, Lincoln, is who I am, who I have always been, and who I always will be.

Francis Bacon offers me a glass of Bollinger:

—Take it, Lincoln, take it. With my compliments.

I feel a twisting, gnawing sensation in my guts. Esurio whispers to me, like a lover:

—Feed me, Lincoln, feed me.

Then, knowing he will get what he wants, his voice rises, triumphant, angry, bouncing off the walls:

—FEED ME, LINCOLN, FEED ME! FEED ME! FEED ME! FEED ME! FEED ME!

A chorus of thousands of voices rises up like a tsunami from the Colony Room.

—FEED HIM! FEED HIM! FEED HIM! FEED HIM!

My head is splitting and I feel blood stuck in my throat and all I want is this drink; to take it, be done with it. I want the real Lincoln Townley back. The Man who can Drink More and Fuck More and Snort More. The Man who almost listened to people telling him to quit. Quit! Never, never, never, never, never. What was I thinking of? *Who* did I think I was?

I drink.

Muriel Belcher walks up to my chair and hands me a small, silver key.

—It's the key to the front door, Cunty. You deserve it.

The Bollinger washes against my throat like holy water and fills me with a deeper, more intense love than I have ever felt before and I am certain, more certain than I have ever been about anything, that I am not alone and that all these people, my *soulmates*, who stand before me, will be with me from now until the end of time and I feel blessed to be who I am, where

I am, right here, with the taste of champagne filling my guts with love. Everyone is going mental and clapping and dancing and cheering and Esurio is flying around the room, laughing like a madman, and I have never been happier.

I hear a different noise, a distant rumbling at first, getting louder and louder, like the approach of a thousand armies, cracking their boots against glass and wood and stone. I cover my ears as the cracking noise gets so loud I want to scream and the room begins to break into millions of pieces. There is glass everywhere and people are cut and screaming with pain. The walls shatter and clumps of masonry are hurled at the guests. In seconds everyone is panicking, as the room breaks apart. I get off my throne just before it's hit by an enormous rock and smashed to pieces. I look up at the carnage and it feels like being on the set of the ultimate disaster movie. Esurio has changed. He is bashing the walls and destroying everything he can with his cane. I notice how big he seems. He towers over the entire scene like an enormous giant and he always has the same, mad, crazy laugh, louder than all the crashing walls and breaking glass and screaming bodies. I see Francis Bacon running until he collapses from exhaustion and his body begins to decompose, his feet and hands first then his arms and legs until he is nothing but a pile of bones on the floor. The poets and painters, musicians, actors and actresses, the homeless and the lost, they are all dying before me and their bodies, ugly and in pain, are slowly turning to dust. I close my eyes and cover my head.

—Please let it all stop! Please!

A voice replies through the carnage:

—Oh, I couldn't possibly do that, Lincoln, not when we're having such fun.

And it goes on for what seems like forever until everything is quiet. So quiet, you could hear a gnat breathe. I open my eyes. Before me, stretching on like a vast desert, are mounds and mounds of dust, glistening in the moonlight and all I can say in my head over and over again are the same two words:

—The horror! The horror!

The air is crisp and there is a wonderful smell of smouldering campfires all around me and I close my eyes to take it all in but, as soon as they are shut, the smell disappears. I feel an intense cold running through my body and when I open my eyes the desert of dust is gone too. I feel someone kicking my feet and I see a Chinese-looking guy and I want to kill him except I can't move. He is saying:

—Move! Move! No lie here. No lie here. People live here.

I look around and I'm lying in the doorway of a shop on Berwick Street.

I can just about make out people moving along the street, ignoring me, except for this Chinese guy who is kicking my feet and who will soon be dead.

—Help move him, to there . . .

I feel myself being carried a few feet before being dropped in another doorway. I look up. This one is covered in metal bars and the shopfront is boarded up. I am holding a bottle of red wine in my hand. I feel inside my jacket pocket for some gear. I can't find anything but when I pull my hand out I lick a few grains off my fingers. Esurio is standing beside me.

—Splendid to have you back with us, Lincoln.

Strange music plays in my head, I see figures dancing and dying, a vast ballroom, fading in and out of my mind.

—What happened to me?

—You just wanted to know . . .

—Know what?

—Not what, Lincoln, *who*.

—I wanted to know . . . who . . .?

—Me, Lincoln, me.

The recollections grow sharper.

—But what about Muriel . . . Francis . . . the Colony Room

—Mine, Lincoln, all mine.

I look at the bottle in my hand.

—How did that get here?

—I bought it for you. In the course of your enlightenment, your little journey into knowledge, I took the opportunity to remind you that life was for living and unless you started living again you would amount to nothing. Nothing whatsoever. But to see you lying here gladdens my heart. I feel sure the Old Lincoln is back with us. Snorting, drinking, taking the ladies into the toilets. I could weep to see you back to your old self. Your True Self, Lincoln.

I finish what's left of the bottle of red wine. I lie on the street listening and watching Soho pass me by. My senses are so sharp and I can hear every sound, it's like I can listen to loads of conversations at the same time and see into people like I have never been able to before. After about half an hour, I get up and walk towards Old Compton Street. I feel a surge of warmth and happiness fizzing through my body. I know I am on the right path and everywhere the signs are spelling it out for me. The last seven days have changed my life. They took me away from who I really am and brought me back again. I feel at home with myself as three words repeat in my head like a mantra: Drink. Coke. Cunt. Drink. Coke. Cunt. Esurio calls them my 'unholy trinity'. I'm not sure what he means but it sounds good. When I get back to the flat there's a Wrap in my bed and I think I'll bang her in the morning when I have had time to rest and think.

The truth is, something else comes into my mind, a conversation I had with Lisa the Pilates teacher the first time I fucked her. I can't remember if it was last week or last month. Maybe last year. I lose track of time. The thing with a Granny is I don't want to leave so quickly when I'm done. I don't even want to talk that much. Just being with them is enough. Usually I go without anything really happening but this time I was with Lisa and she told me this story:

—In a previous life, the Buddha was a very pious monk and one day he and a young novice came to a river where a woman was standing unable to cross because the water was moving too fast. She asked the monk to help her cross, so he lifted her onto his back and carried her to the other side. She thanked him and left. For the rest of the day the monk and the novice walked in silence. When the monk asked the novice a question he refused to answer. That night, as they sat around a small fire, the monk asked the novice what was troubling him.

'Now that you ask, Master, it is the woman. You know it is forbidden for a holy man to touch the body of a woman and yet you carried her across the river.'

'That's true,' the monk replied. 'I did carry her but I let her go many hours ago. You have been carrying her ever since.'

I don't know why that comes into my head as I sit on my bed in Old Compton Street. I don't really care. It just popped up. I think:

—Maybe it's the truth.

I don't understand that thought.

I feel something in my jacket pocket. I pull it out. It's a

silver key. I don't know where it came from. I put it in my bedside table and think:

—I wonder what it fits.

I lie down and as soon as my head hits the pillow I am asleep.

A Party in Cannes

April–May 2010

The first time you fall, it's bad. The second time, it's worse than you can ever imagine. I remember watching a documentary about a guy on Death Row. When the day of his execution came, he had been praying for hours and got himself ready to walk to the execution chamber. They filmed him leaving his cell for the last time. He was calm and prepared to die. Then he got a reprieve. A last-minute appeal was being heard. So he went back to his cell and waited. The appeal failed. The second time he left his cell he had to be dragged, sweating and screaming, to the execution chamber. That's what the second time does. It's always worse.

It's a warm spring afternoon and Soho seems darker than ever. I am drunk when I bump into John in a cafe in Greek Street. He can see how I am but he asks me anyway. I tell him things are good. The Club is doing well. I am holding myself together. He nods and I tell him:

—The meetings weren't for me. I feel for me it's better to find my own way through this.

He nods again and says something I don't hear, then we shake hands and I make my way to the Soho Hotel. I've got a room booked. Two Wraps, a Regular and a Paid-For. I pound the living daylights out of them and with every thrust I sink deeper into a dark pit. As soon as I begin pounding I want it to be over. To be somewhere, anywhere, other than in this hotel room. As I'm pounding I think:

—Too much sex is more tedious than celibacy.

Esurio is at the bottom of the bed, trying to get the best angle to see into as many holes as he can at the same time. At one point he runs his tongue up a Wrap's thigh and blows into her pussy. I'm amazed how narrow and pointed his tongue is. The Wrap shudders and wonders how I do it. He senses what I'm thinking:

—The monastic life is not for you, Lincoln.

I imagine how many paintings I might do if I wasn't banging all the time.

—And if you think about how many paintings you might create in a cloister, the answer will be none. Not a single one. Great art and excess are the perfect bedfellows. The one cannot live without the other.

When I'm done I snort a few lines off their buttocks and leave. I take a deep breath as I walk out onto Dean Street. I try to take in some air but it is too thick and gooey for me to inhale. I make a list in my head of important things I know:

IMPORTANT THINGS I KNOW

1. I know what is bad for me
2. I can know what is bad for me and still do it
3. I am not Immortal
4. Sex is overrated
5. The second fall is always worse than the first

I stop at five and create another list of important things I believe:

IMPORTANT THINGS I BELIEVE

1. However bad it gets, there's always time to recover
2. I can take more than other men because I am stronger
3. If I run fast enough I can cheat death
4. I can't live without sex
5. The worse it gets, the more I'll prove everybody wrong

I turn the two lists around in my head, trying to use one to make sense of the other when I almost fall down a hole in the ground. Luckily a workman shouts at me as I knock the red and white barrier down. I don't feel a thing as I bash into it, but the shout draws me out of myself and I'm standing a couple of feet away from a hole the men have dug to work on some pipes. I want to kill the man for shouting at me. Then I'm grateful until the anger rises in me again. I'm about to walk away when I look down into the hole. I think it's strange that I can't see any pipes. It's dark and seems to go on forever. A man asks me if I am OK. I say yes and thank him. He steps into the hole and I grab his arm to stop him from falling.

—Careful! It's very deep!

He stands in the hole, his feet on the ground and his entire upper body above street level. He smiles at me. I have seen that smile before when an ambulance crew came to Frith Street to take a guy away who had been blessing passing cars for the best part of an afternoon.

The second fall is much worse.

When I get to The Office, the boys are there. It's a few weeks until the Cannes Film Festival and Terry is panicking. He hasn't got enough money to go. Or rather, he hasn't got enough money to go, get smashed and get laid. Toby is his last chance. He is on his seventh shot and third line of coke and staring at his phone on the table.

—Ring, you fucker, ring!

I am sitting on the next table with Maynard and Simon. Maynard shakes his head and says:

—Look, Terry, we're all going anyway. It doesn't matter too much if—

—Doesn't fucking matter! Of course it matters. Fifty grand from Toby turns a film festival into an orgy.

The phone rings. Terry snatches it off the table.

—Hi, Toby, how's things? Great. Thought anymore about the Fund? Yes, I see, I can understand why you might want to wait. Shame about missing out on Cannes, though . . . Oh, sorry, I thought you knew. Only investors in the Fund get to Cannes . . . It would be good if you could. Cannes is a great place to network . . . Yes, that's right. I've got several Film Funds off the ground in Cannes . . . I'm thinking Art-House. I'm seeing Werner . . . Herzog. And Thomas . . . Vinterberg . . . but I don't want to rule out something more mainstream, either, so I'll certainly be catching up with Ridley while I'm there . . . Scott . . . Anyone you'd like to see? Pity you can't get the money to me before because she'll be there and I can guarantee you an introduction. Yes, honestly. Guaranteed. I promise . . . You will, that's wonderful!

The boys punch the air.

—. . . and of course cash is great. Just bring it round tomorrow . . .

They stand up and start cheering.

—. . . Oh, that's just the crowd, Toby. I'm at a premiere and Charlize Theron just walked in. Look, I've got to go, she's calling me over . . . You will, Toby, you will. See you tomorrow.

Terry punches the air. Maynard gives him a massive bear hug. Everyone in the restaurant seems to be cheering.

Maynard unhooks himself from Terry. He is a worrier and looks concerned.

—What did you promise him, Terry?

—Oh, nothing much.

—Terry, what did you promise him?

—I just told him he could join me and Megan Fox for dinner.

—What the fuck did you tell him that for?

—How else was I supposed to get the money? It closed the deal, didn't it?

—Great. We're going to have some upper-class knob hanging around all week waiting for dinner with Megan fucking Fox!

—Look, Maynard, by the end of the first day, he isn't going to know where he is, who he is, what fucking planet he lives on. I could put Dame Edna Everage on top of him and tell him it's Megan Fox and he'll be the happiest man in Cannes.

Esurio is delighted.

—Bit of sun is exactly what you need right now, Lincoln. Go to Cannes and soak it up.

He's right. Since the Grand Ball I haven't felt myself. It's like I've been stalked by a Terrible Loneliness and whatever I take I can't seem to get rid of it. Perhaps I don't even care whether I live or die. It's like I've lost hope but I don't even know what I was hoping for. More? More of what? I used to crave pleasure. In recent days, it seems all my energy is spent taking the pain away. I am, however, certain there is a point, a *quantity* of booze and gear, where I will feel better. I just haven't reached it yet.

—Then just keep going, Lincoln. You'll know it when you get there.

—I will. Too fucking right I will.

Three weeks later, I'm sitting next to Toby on the flight to Cannes. Somewhere in the back of the plane Terry, Steve, Maynard and Simon are asleep.

—Goody good.

I've just told Toby to expect the best time of his life. He is perhaps thirty. And he has a quiff. I feel sorry for him. I'm shaking from last night. To calm my nerves I took a line and half-a-dozen shots before we took off. But it's not enough. If I've got to sit next to someone who says 'goody good' I haven't a fucking clue what 'enough' would be. I close my eyes.

—So, Lincoln, are you looking forward to the festival?

I don't want to talk. I don't want any contact with anyone.

—Yeah, it'll be great.

—Hope so. My good friend Burgess went once. Had a wonderful time. Can't wait to meet Megan.

He digs me in the ribs. I open my eyes and sit on my hands. They are fighting against the pressure, willing me to release them and let them knock his teeth out. One of them escapes and is waving wildly in the air.

—It's OK. I'll call her. Stewardess? Here, please!

She arrives as my arm is inches from his mouth.

—Another vodka, sir?

—Er, yeah. OK.

Perhaps six hours later we are in a theatre in Cannes watching some Scandinavian film. It has subtitles. I guess it's Scandinavian because every word seems to end in a vowel. I've no idea what the film is about. I can't even see the screen. Occasionally I pop into the toilets to vomit. At the end the director gets on the stage but I haven't a clue what he is talking about. I think it's Tuesday and Terry's got a party organised at our villa on Thursday. I need another drink. Another line.

Wednesday disappears. On Thursday morning I wake up with three Wraps in my bed. Out on the balcony I can see Toby puking on his dressing gown. I shout at him:

—Tonight, Toby, it's Megan night!

—Goo . . .

He collapses on the floor. I guess he'll be out until the afternoon.

The bedside table is laced with coke. I take it. The Wraps are awake now.

—You could have left some for us.

I think that's the stupidest thing I have ever heard. I am on my phone all morning. It was my job to organise twenty-five Wraps and get them to the villa. Or rather it was Tina's job. I gave her two grand to sort it out. Terry has been on my back. He's got some film guys coming over for the party.

—Promise me, Lincoln, the girls will be there. I'm relying on you.

I call Tina. We're eight short.

—Sorry, Lincoln. They were all here yesterday but they seem to have disappeared.

—Disappeared! How can you lose eight girls in twenty-four hours?!

I remember where we are and I'm relieved we've only lost eight. I kick everyone out of the flat. The boys carry Toby into the taxi still in his dressing gown. By late evening the villa is ready. We found four of the girls and Tina went around Cannes and picked up another five. One up on the deal! I walk through the villa. Jim, the mixologist, is set up by the pool. He's a genius. His cocktails have appeared on the cover of *Vanity Fair* and he can stay sober long enough for the Wraps to take the guests beyond the point where they might notice a drop in standards.

Ten-thirty. The guests begin to arrive. I greet them with a firm handshake. I am glad I took another line and a couple of shots to steady myself. Within an hour the ground floor of the villa is packed with men. Average age: forty. Average income: more than even I could dream of. Wraps are everywhere. Smart. No G-strings. They could be old money at Ascot. It takes maybe an hour, a few lines of coke, Jeroboams of Cristal Champagne, some Cuban cigars and endless shots of Kauffman vodka for the carnage to begin.

My parties work because I know how men work. You can have all the money in the world but when the girls start working you're a pauper who doesn't even own his own mind. I smile as I watch the men begin to fight. A thick-set guy in a light-blue jacket and matching shoes puts twenty grand behind the bar. Another guy puts thirty. In every room some guy is having his cock sucked. The pool is full of naked girls. I call Terry over.

—Where are the boys?

—Upstairs I think.

—Toby?

—Fucked.

—Great, let's go up to my room.

I signal to six Wraps. They follow me up the stairs. When we get to my bedroom, everyone is there. They are all fucked. Toby is slumped against the wardrobe. Simon is taking a line off the coffee table and smiling.

—At least he's getting his money's worth!

Within minutes the girls are naked. So am I. I'm leaning against the wall. My cock is hard. Toby opens his eyes and sees the girls. Then he catches a glimpse of my cock. He squints, unsure of what he is looking at. Terry shouts at him:

—Hey, Toby, Megan's come to see you.

One of the Wraps walks over to him and runs her hands through his quiff.

—Hi, I'm Megan …

She plays the script to perfection.

—Oh, my God, no …

He crawls into the wardrobe and pulls the door behind him.

—What's the matter with him?

—He's just a bit star-struck.

As I'm fucking, I hear a banging noise coming from inside the wardrobe then a hand coming out and touching the Wrap's arse. It goes back inside the wardrobe. More banging. Out it comes again. The whole wardrobe is shaking. He really is an upper-class wanker.

The next day the blossom outside my bedroom is radiant. Life after death is more beautiful than I ever imagined. The villa is wrecked. Naked bodies litter the floor. I walk over to the balcony and check the pool for any dead ones. All clear.

A foot is hanging out of the wardrobe. I open the door. Toby is unconscious, his hand still holding his cock. He moans, dribbles from the left side of his mouth and then goes quiet. Another happy investor.

I go out for a run. The sun is hot on my back and the world is strangely normal. As I pound along the beach I start crying. I don't know where the tears come from. They just appear. I keep running. After perhaps five miles, I feel sick and my heart is screaming but I can't stop. I want to die, sink under the sand with the sun on my back and the sea blue and beautiful. There's only one thing worse than being a drunk and that's those short gaps between one binge and the next, where a thin sliver of reality breaks through and I can see what I have become. I know there is no way back for me now, so I will keep running until I collapse and maybe some passer-by will pick me up and take me home. Or leave me in the gutter.

When I get back to the villa, I join Maynard for a drink on a balcony overlooking the sea. His face is wobbling like one of those nodding donkeys my Dad used to have in his car. Except this is a slow wobble, as if the mechanism moving the head is grinding to a halt. He doesn't acknowledge me when I sit next to him. His head finally stops moving. I notice he has a whisky in his hand. His hand is still and his eyes are closed.

—Maynard . . . it's me, Lincoln. Maynard! Are you dead?

I'm relieved when he grunts. I imagine he has been sitting here for hours. I take the glass from his hand and, as the alcohol hits my throat, I am calm again. I look at Maynard's face baking in the sun. He is sweating. He looks ill, and as I stare at him I feel a rush of love. Not the eternal love one drunk has for another. A deeper love. Compassion. As if all I want in this moment is for him to get up off the chair, walk down to the beach and just keep going. Keep moving until he is so far away he can't be rerouted back to The Office. More than anyone I want Maynard to break free from all the shit. He is kind and funny. But above all, he is a man gifted with talent and I love him enough to hate him for wasting it.

His right hand, locked into an empty grip where the whisky once was, moves. I slip the empty glass back into his hand. It takes him a few moments to notice the absence of liquid in his mouth. He opens his eyes. They are red and laced with death.

—Whe ... where ...

Giving up on the possibility of speech, he gestures with his head towards the empty hand.

—Gone, Maynard. It's all gone.

He is unconscious again before I reply.

We must have got back to London because I'm lying on my bed in Old Compton Street. I think it's mid-afternoon. I need a drink. Now. I can hear Esurio pacing outside on the landing. I want him to go away. I need to sleep. I close my eyes and, as I feel myself drifting off, he storms into the bedroom and begins having a real go at me.

—Get up! Now! I'm hungry, Lincoln, and all you can do is lie here feeling sorry for yourself. I'm not having it. Get up now!

—Give me an hour, just one hour ...

—No! Time's up. We're going out now.

I imagine my hands around his throat, squeezing the life out of him. He knows what I'm thinking and laughs at me. I put my hands over my ears and he prods me with his cane. I lunge out of the bed but whichever way I turn he is faster than me. I punch a hole in the wall in frustration. He laughs. The angrier I become, the funnier he finds it. He thrives on it.

Ever since the Grand Ball, Esurio has changed. He can still be funny and charming, loving even, but most times he bullies me. He used to get aggressive now and then but these days he is more . . . contemptuous. That's the word. He treats me like the dirt on his silver-buckled shoe. I wonder what this means and I make a mental note of six possible reasons for this change:

1. He believes he doesn't have to try anymore.
2. He thinks I'm weak.
3. He sees that I have surrendered.
4. He wants to leave me.
5. He can't end our relationship until it reaches its natural conclusion.
6. He is frustrated at being stuck with me.

It occurs to me that these are really all one reason. All I am certain of is that he has changed and we are driving on to wherever he wants to take us. I am a passenger and I am resigned to what I have become. There was a time when I was able to do deals with him. He would give me a few hours' rest in return for a night in the 'red zone'. Now he won't even do that. He says:

—I only deal when I have to. You understand sales, Lincoln. When the deal is closed, never give anything away and I do not have to give you anything anymore.

As I check my handkerchief in the mirror, I know he is too strong for me. Perhaps he always was and he was playing with me, like a cat toying with a mouse. There is entertainment value in the moments before an execution. I read once about why they used to hang, draw and quarter people. It wasn't because they wanted to kill the prisoner. It was to keep him alive long enough for the mob to enjoy the pain. When I am done adjusting my jacket, I catch Esurio's reflection in the mirror and let out a scream. His face is covered in a black hood and he is holding an axe. Beside him on the floor is a rack. When I turn, the rack is gone and he is back to his normal self:

—Had you worried there, didn't I?

He is a bully. Too strong for me to control. There are no more deals to be done. Where he goes, I will go. Where he sleeps, I will sleep. I will keep doing this even though I know he will tire of me. One day, I know he will devour me. I am powerless before him and he will finish with me at a time of his own choosing. For now, I'm good sport. I make him laugh. I feed him. But I sense he is growing tired of me, and when I am weak and pathetic, when my blood is made of booze and my cock limp, he will throw me into a gutter on Dean Street and move on to other bodies. That's the end game. Like cancer he will eat away at me until there's nothing left. We both know the rules. But we are not there yet. For now, I can borrow time on condition that the next fuck-up, the next ridiculous dream, is more costly than the one that came before it. Esurio is without mercy. I hate him.

I'm also having more nightmares than usual and I'm seeing things. I leave the flat and make my way to The Office. At the corner of Old Compton Street and Dean Street, people's faces begin to twist and melt like a Francis Bacon painting, and when I walk past a woman in rags in a boarded-up doorway, I recognise her. Her name is Edie and she spent years living on the streets until she died a month after I moved to Soho. A man walks up to me and asks me the time. When I look up to answer him, he is no longer there. These people are my Familiars. They come. They go.

—Faster, Lincoln, faster!

Esurio is driving me on, prodding me in the back with his cane. I dream of killing him, of stuffing his cane so far up his arse it comes out of his mouth. But I know I can't. I need him. And he knows I need him. And so we walk up to the entrance to The Office, joined at the hip, Siamese twins who will stay together until he decides to split us apart and then one of us will die:

—And remember, Lincoln, it won't be me.

I order a bottle of Rioja and go straight down to the toilets to take some lines. When I come back up, Esurio is waiting for me at the table, holding a glass of absinthe. He isn't smiling:

—Now entertain me, Lincoln, entertain me!

Darkness in Soho

June 2010. 3 a.m.

The basement of the Dirty Dance Strip Club is full of punters and Eastern European Wraps. The music is banging on the inside of my head and everything is twisting and gnawing. I feel sick. I go into a toilet cubicle and push the seat down. I put so much gear on it, the whole seat turns white. As I snort it, Esurio has his boot on my neck, pressing it down so I have to use all my strength to keep my nose high enough to snort.

—You're a strong man, Lincoln, very strong.

He used to say that with sincerity. Now his voice is laced with derision. When I'm done, the sweat is pouring down my face and my heart is howling like a caged wolf. Esurio opens the door for me back into the basement and makes an exaggerated gesture with his cane, to bloat his sense of generosity. I ignore him and, as I walk through the door, he drops his cane to the ground and I fall over it. A couple of Wraps rush over and help me to my feet. When their hands touch the shoulder of my jacket and I feel their fingers pressing gently into my flesh, I want to burst into tears. It's a touch that only a woman can give and perhaps only a desperate, drunken man can understand what it means.

When I'm back on my feet I go with the Wraps to a corner away from the bar. They are both stunning, with long black hair, one slightly darker than the other. I guess they are both Russian. They are dressed in bras and G-strings. One black, one white. I need a drink. Another line. One of the Wraps leans over towards me and whispers into my ear. I think she says:

—You like my ass?

I don't acknowledge her, but she pushes my hand under her buttocks and guides my index finger into her arse. And I sit there. A vodka tonic in one hand. Darkness like I have never felt before in the other. The entire basement seems to disappear and everything is black. I can feel my finger moving about inside her, foraging, but I've lost all sense of what it's doing there or what I'm looking for. In the past, the King of Soho would have taken this arse as his Divine Right and displayed it to the world. Now ...

—You not want?

The Wrap looks at me and eases my finger out. It's the same look I saw in her eyes when she picked me off the floor. She's right. I not want. Anything.

8 a.m.

I wake up sitting in a Ferrari in Mayfair, just around the corner from Bar 45. I borrowed it yesterday from a dealership. The manager is a regular at The Club. I look after him and occasionally he sorts me out a car as a thank you. I think I was meant to be taking a Swedish Wrap out in it but it never happened and now I don't know how I got here or how long I have been asleep. I lift my hands up. They're shaking. My whole body is shaking. I have a meeting with The Boss in half an hour and I need to get to The Club. I want to puke. I wretch a few times but nothing comes up. I look at my hands again. Shaking. Out of control. I think:

—I can't let The Boss see me like this.

Then I think:

—One line will sort it out.

I pull some gear out of my jacket. I am sobbing like a fucking baby as I snort it off the dashboard. When it's all up my nose I look at my watch. I have ten minutes to get to The Club. I turn the keys in the ignition. The engine purrs. My foot hits the accelerator and then I hesitate. Esurio is tapping his cane on the windscreen and shouting at me:

—Drive, you wretch, drive!

I turn the engine off, jump out of the car and start sprinting down Curzon Street. I am delirious. Shouting at no one:

—Fuck you!

I'm sprinting across Berkeley Square, heading towards Conduit Street, and all I can hear above the city and the traffic is his laugh. It bounces around my head and when I press my hands up to my ears to block it out, it just gets louder. The laughter is coming from somewhere deep *inside* me. I pull at my head, trying to tear it out but still it goes on. People look at me like I'm insane. I *am* insane. By the time I turn into Berwick Street, my entire body is creaking like the hull of a sinking ship. I feel death is close. Closer than I have ever felt it before. I am almost ready to surrender, to let it take me, do what it wants with me, anything to make the pain go away. At the furthest point of this feeling, I feel her touch again on my shoulder: the Russian Wrap, soft, feminine, maternal. Kind.

Kinder than I deserve. It carries me to The Club. I am on time. I stumble into The Office and grip the door to hold me up. The sweat has passed through my shirt and the inside of my jacket is soaking wet. The Boss looks up from his desk. I hate what I see in his face: pity.

He asks the other people in The Office to give us a few moments. I can't look him in the eye. I wish he was angry. I think:

I'll provoke him, force him to be angry with me.

I can't. I have too much love and respect for him. He goes easy on me:

—You've broken our deal but I won't cut your money down to the floor. I'll take you back to what you were on before I gave you the rise.

—Thanks, Boss.

—Please look after yourself. You're a top man. Don't waste it. Go home, get yourself cleaned up and we'll reschedule the meeting.

I get up to leave and, as I do, he adds:

—What you do on the outside is your business, but if I catch you taking drugs in any of the clubs I'll sack you straight away.

—I know. Thanks for that, too.

The rest of the day disappears in a nightmare of drink, coke and cunt. Through all the madness I notice something happening inside me. It's a familiar feeling, a toxic mix of pain and fury, one that has come and gone in waves as long as I can remember, but now it is unleashed, wild and howling, incapable of restraint.

Like all violent urges it is a defence against an attack, real or imagined, on me or those that I love and, after Dad died, I began to lose control over it. When I was sixteen, my Mum, still lost in grief, became friends with a man called Bob. I didn't have any feelings towards Bob. I just wanted my Mum to be happy. If he was kind to her then he was OK by me. He wasn't kind to her. He piled his stuff in her garage and wouldn't move it. I asked my Mum if she wanted me to sort it out for her. She said:

—Yes.

An instant later, she realised what she had done and said:

—No.

But by then I was on my way to the model shop he owned with a baseball bat in my hand. I opened the door, flipped the 'Open' sign to 'Closed', walked passed battleships and Spitfires and thumped the counter with the baseball bat. I was a kid and this man in his mid-forties fell to his knees and started crying.

—Please don't hurt me, please don't hurt me . . .

—You've got until Saturday to get your stuff out of the garage. If it's still there when I go to Mum's on Sunday, I'll come back for you.

A strange, gloved hand, attached to a ghostly arm and the faint outline of a body, picked the baseball bat off the counter and passed it to me. I think I heard a voice:

—Well done, Lincoln, well done!

The stuff was gone from the garage the next day.

Walking away from The Club after the meeting, I think about Bob and my mind takes me back to that shop and everything looks the same as I remember it, except this time I am beating him with the baseball bat until his head explodes and when I'm done I destroy the fucking shop and everything in it. When the place is wrecked I catch my reflection in a cracked mirror on the wall behind the counter. My face is red and covered in blood. It must be a distortion caused by the broken glass. I look again. The same image. My throat is cut and a gloved hand pulls a knife away from my neck. Before I fall to the ground I am already dead. I have been dead for some time. I doubt whether I have ever truly been alive, so I ask my Mum:

—How do you know you're alive?

She looks at me as if I'm crazy:

—What sort of question is that? You wouldn't still be here if you weren't alive.

I know, with absolute certainty, she is wrong.

The Next Day

What used to give me pleasure now seems only to relieve the pain but I have an idea in my head that if I keep taking more, I will feel more like my Old Self. It is not that I am afraid of pain. It's just that there are two types of pain. I call them Shallow and Deep. I am used to the first one and I know I can deal with it. The second one is new and scares the shit out of me. Here's an example of me dealing with Shallow Pain:

I was in my early thirties on a holiday in Paris with my girl-friend. I had been having problems with one of my back teeth for some time and, on our third night in Paris, I managed to break it. Not chip it. Break it. The nerves were exposed and the pain was fucking unbelievable. I took a painkiller. It got worse. After my sixth tablet I gave up. My girlfriend said:

—You need to get to an emergency dentist immediately.

By now the pain had taken hold of my life. Nothing else mattered. I had to deal with it now.

—I haven't got time. I'll sort it out now.

—How are you going to do that?

—Get my toothbrush.

—Your toothbrush?

—Just get it now!

I broke the toothbrush in half and pressed the broken end of the handle half against the door with the smooth end facing out. I asked my girlfriend to move the door in and out slowly so I could align the smooth end to hit my broken tooth when the door was shut. When I was certain the angles were correct I gripped the toothbrush and said to her:

—When I shout 'Slam', you slam the door shut as hard as you can.

—But . . .

—No fucking 'buts'. Do it!

She opened the door as wide as was possible to enable me to keep my grip on the toothbrush.

Slam!

I felt a crack as the toothbrush bashed into the enamel and exposed nerves of the tooth. I felt a searing pain rip through every cell of my body. My mouth was like an exploding volcano of hot, molten agony. The tooth had shifted but was still hanging on. Blood was dripping out of my mouth onto my shirt and hands.

—Again.

—What?

—Again!

As soon as the door was opened to the same distance as the first time, I screamed:

Slam!

This time the toothbrush knocked the tooth out of my

mouth. There was blood everywhere. I could still feel bits of root dangling in my mouth. I forced three fingers into the fleshy remnants of my tooth socket and tugged and twisted and pulled until I was sure everything was out. My girlfriend was crying:

—That's horrible!

I went to look in the mirror. I lifted my cheek to see the damage. All traces of the tooth were gone. I washed my mouth out and smiled. That's the thing about Shallow Pain: you know what causes it and you know it will pass.

Deep Pain is more mysterious. It's impossible to get a grip on what's causing it because it seems to be everywhere all at once, like it defines who you are. You can feel strong and fit and healthy and still be riddled with Deep Pain. Shallow Pain takes over a part of your body. Deep Pain takes over your soul, and I think the only way to cure Deep Pain is to kill your soul.

So it's the Next Day and I am in a jazz club. I can't be sure of the time because I am bollocksed. I am not happy because I haven't had a Happy Day since the Grand Ball. Nor have I seen the sun. Not even in Cannes. All the boys from The Office are in the club and when Geoff, the floor manager, sees me, he points them out to me at the bar. I walk over and Maynard, Terry and Simon are messing about with a couple of Wraps. I have done this a hundred times and I know the routine. Except this time it's different. The Wraps are as available as they always are, but I am on a different journey now. I want annihilation. To wipe myself out. It's the only way I can be stopped and I'm waiting for an opportunity. I have only needed a few minutes of patience when a guy standing next to us at the bar slaps one of the Wraps on her arse. I say:

—Don't do that.

He replies:

—I'll do whatever I want.

And when I go to pick my glass off the bar, he says:

—It's my drink. Fucking leave it alone, arsehole!

I take it and wait. Nothing. I turn away and a few seconds later I hear him call the Wrap a 'slapper' to his mates and he is pointing at me and saying:

—It's the only bird a bald-headed cunt like that can get . . .

I leave my glass on the bar and go down a narrow flight of stairs to the toilet. I have taken a line or two off the toilet seat and I am pissing in a urinal when the guy at the bar walks into the toilet and heads straight for me. I look just past his left shoulder to distract him and when he buys it, I punch him full force on the side of the face. He falls to the ground like he has been shot. He is unconscious. Maybe dead. I *hope* he is dead, but after a few moments I hear him groan. It's the last thing I hear before the door to the toilet is stormed by police officers. I don't know how many. I get my fists ready and start punching wildly. One of them grabs me from behind and I headbutt him. I hear his nose crack and blood drops over my shoulder and onto my cock. I think:

—Fuck me! My cock's still out.

I make a bolt for the door when I feel my body rising off the ground and all I can see is a blinding, white light. I feel like *It is Accomplished*. Over. The floating, the white light, this is how I imagined it to be. I wait for the procession of dead relatives when I feel a bang on my face as it hits the fluorescent lights of the toilet. There is glass everywhere and the cop whose nose bled on my cock is back on his feet. He says:

—You're in fucking trouble now, sunshine!

More cops rush down the stairs into the bathroom and the

cop whose nose bled on my cock turns me face down and two, maybe three, other cops begin dragging me feet first up the wooden stairs. With every step my head thumps against the wood. I'm screaming, kicking, spitting, shouting, as my head bangs harder on the stairs until I hear it crack. I think my skull is about to split open when I'm dragged through a door back into the bar and lifted so high in the air by the cops, my face almost touches the ceiling. I am borne above the crowd, a *Martyr to Nothingness*, my cock swinging in the light like a Holy Staff, until I feel the cold night air on my face and I'm thrown into the back of a meat-wagon. Bound by my hands and feet, I writhe like a fish on the floor of the van, waiting for my air to expire and I'm released only when I am placed in a cell at a local Police Station. As soon as the cell door shuts behind me, I rush at the door and pound it with my shoulder. I force bits of my face out of the small barred area at the top of the cell door:

—Fuck you! Fuck you!

The door opens and three cops enter. I rush at them, fists flying. They jump on me and keep me face down on the floor of the cell and, when I think I'm going to pass out, another cop enters, his hands and arms gloved up to the elbow:

—Strip him! I'm going to search him for drugs!

I am instantly quiet and sober. I raise my hands in a gesture of submission. I say:

—Please don't. I'm sorry, I'll be OK now.

The cops back off. They look stunned, convinced some benign *doppelgänger* has taken over my body, and the new cop with the gloves looks at me and backs off. They leave me alone in the cell. I am shocked that I stopped, that I was *able* to stop, that some remote part of my unconscious mind was still capable of processing enough information to get me to act on it. I assume it must be something primal in a man, the thought of a man's hand up your arse, a *hostile* man's hand, pulling at your insides, that reminds you there is more to life than death. There is the humiliation that precedes death and that is the greater horror.

I lie down on the bed and look up at the bare ceiling. I am about to fall asleep when I hear a tapping on the cell floor. I turn over, thinking it will go away. It gets louder. I sit up and Esurio is standing before me, banging his cane against the wall above my head.

—You're a coward, Lincoln. Losing your fight like that. I'm appalled at you.

—What did you expect me to do?

—I expect nothing of you anymore, Lincoln, absolutely nothing. How many people do you think I know intimately, very intimately, as if they were my own flesh and blood, that have found themselves in positions like this, and they would have died in this cell, *died* rather retreat in fear?

—Leave me alone. I want to get some sleep.

—Never! What makes you think you are worth anything, Lincoln, let alone a sleep from which you fully intend to wake up?

I ignore him.

—Answer me!

I feel his cane fall across my back with a huge thud. I wince and stand up to face him. He is already behind me in the far corner of the cell, smiling with contempt.

—Tell me, who would miss you, Lincoln, if you were carried out of this cell in a body bag? Who? Your mother? I don't think so. You've hardly been a good son, have you? *You're* not the son she wanted. She wanted a boy who'd keep his nose clean, stick around with her, drink more tea than alcohol. Not you, is it? And what about your son, Lewis? So you've paid a bit of maintenance and taken him to fun fairs as a five-year-old. Bravo! Do you really think he'd miss a Dad who doesn't stick around for more than three days in a row? And your own father, well he had enough of you by the time you were a teenager, so he went on holiday to a caravan park in Kent and never bothered coming home . . .

I kick the wall in fury over and over again until I think I can hear my bones cracking.

— . . . And, oh yes, there's your mates. Friends, I believe you call them. Well, let's be honest, you'd be worth a drink to them, perhaps even a toast *In Memory of Lincoln*, but they will forget you before the first glass is empty. So what is your life worth, Lincoln?

I am hunched up in a ball, rocking, crying.

—Nothing, I'm not worth anything. My life is a piece of piss.

Esurio roars, his voice echoing as it bounces off the cell walls:

—Then end it! End it! End it!

I put my hands behind my neck and pull my face down into my knees. I pull as hard as I can, waiting for my neck to break. I am worth Nothing. Not even to my mother, my father, my son. I promise, I deliver, then I stop delivering and promise some more, and so it goes on. I release my neck. I don't even have the courage to break it.

—How dare you defy me and continue to breathe! If that is your attitude, you will never rest again . . .

I look up at Esurio and, as I watch him, great tufts of black hair force their way through his clothes, tearing the fabric to shreds. His limbs and torso change their shape and he drops onto all fours, lowers his face, and, when he lifts it, the transformation is complete. A mad, rabid dog – bigger, wilder than any wolf I have ever seen – stands a few feet away from me, clumps of saliva oozing from its mouth and falling onto the cell floor. I press my back against the wall. The creature moves forward, fixing me with its gaze. It barks and roars at me, hunching back as if it's about to leap at me, before it withdraws and circles the cell, taunting me, waiting patiently for me to offer myself to its jaws. On all fours, it stands perhaps five feet tall and I wonder what it would be like to rush at its mouth and let it rip me to pieces. But I'm a coward, too weak to surrender, and so I sit, hour after hour, all through the night, helpless. At first, I shout at the door, hoping the cops might hear me. They don't. I guess they can't. And even if they could, what would they do? What is my life worth to them? All night it stalks me. It is perhaps about sunrise when I notice for the first time a bottle of vodka standing against the wall of the cell. Between the bottle and me, sits the creature. I get on my knees:

—Please, please, just one mouthful, just one and I promise I'll leave the rest . . .

Then:

—Fuck you! Let me have a fucking drink! I NEED A DRINK!

This goes on for what seems like an eternity, broken up by moments where I am almost asleep. Almost. The creature watches my eyes close from exhaustion and, just as I am on the verge of passing into unconsciousness, it howls and roars and presses up so close to me I can feel the heat and smell of its breath.

When the cell door opens, it is seven in the morning. Two cops come in. One of them says:

—You were making a lot of noise in here last night. We looked in at you a few times and you were hunched in a ball in the corner. Is everything all right?

—Does it look like it is?

When they release me, they remind me I have been charged with assaulting a police officer. On the way out, Esurio smiles at me:

—Quite a night, Lincoln.

—There's been plenty of them.

—I have no doubt there will be many more. I predict this place, let's christen it the Charing Cross Hotel, will become like a holiday home to you. The more desperate a man gets, the more his life unravels like a ball of string, and yours is rolling away nicely, Lincoln, very nicely indeed.

The Charing Cross Hotel

July–August 2010

This is my Summer of Hate. I'm pounding more, drinking more, snorting more, running more, lifting more, than I ever thought possible. I'm heading for a *World Record in Pointless Endurance* and I'm certain that one day my heart will explode. This will be a heart attack unlike any other. I have visions of my heart bursting through my ribcage and spreading bits of flesh the length and breadth of Dean Street. During the Summer of Hate, I am angrier than ever, with my head full of images of what I would like to do to people who cross me, and my concept of 'cross' is VERY broad. Here's a few examples:

- A cyclist passes too close to me when I'm walking along the pavement on Wardour Street and I want to rip his head off and stick it on the spokes of his bicycle wheel.
- A man collecting for charity on Leicester Square taps me on the head with a giant, inflatable banana as I walk past him. I grab him by the throat and threaten to hang him from a pole at The Club.

- A newsagent on Beak Street short-changes me and later that day I go back and threaten to stuff every newspaper in his shop up his arse.
- I try to withdraw some money from my Santander account and the hole-in-the-wall doesn't work, so I go into the branch but I am too drunk to understand what the man behind the counter is telling me, so I punch the counter and when he asks me to stop I tell him I wish his face was the counter. Three security guards escort me off the premises.

None of these incidents ends in a stay at the Charing Cross Hotel. These do:

The Terminator Incident
It's about three in the morning and I'm coming out of The Club. A woman brushes passed me and distracts me, while a man grabs my wrist. By the time I notice he has stolen my Rolex, he is already running down the road. I'm drunk, so I take a deep breath before removing my jacket and shirt and handing them to the Wrap I am with. I begin jogging slowly at first, then gradually I speed up until I'm sprinting after him. He is younger than me, maybe mid-twenties, slim and fit, but he has never been chased by anyone like me before. I am relentless and, at first, I am maybe three hundred yards behind him. After a few minutes of running, it's down to fifty, and I can see him looking over his shoulder at a topless maniac that he knows will catch him and kill him. He starts squealing from fear because his energy is failing while mine is getting stronger, so he turns back and shouts:

—Look! Look! I'll leave it on the corner here . . .

He leaves it on the ground, keeps running, and looks over his shoulder to make sure I pick up the watch and stop chasing him. I do stop, pick up the watch, put it back on my wrist and then go after him again. He is now in a blind panic until he finds himself back on same road he started on, where he drops to his knees. I don't know what he says because I don't even slow down as I approach him, pull my fist back and knock him out with a single blow to the mouth. I am looking at my hand and wondering what's embedded in it when I realise it's one of his teeth. As I pull it out and throw it on the floor, a police car pulls up alongside me. It was parked on the opposite side of the road when I hit him. I collect my shirt and jacket from the Wrap and get a free lift to the Charing Cross Hotel.

Length of Stay:	4 hours
Room Service:	1 weak tea and a glass of water
Bill:	A caution
Rating:	★★★

The Tea Towel Incident

It's one of those balmy summer evenings and I'm downstairs in the Archer Street Wine Bar with the boys where a DJ is playing a '70s retrospective. For once, my mood is merely Dark as opposed to Pitch Black. That changes when a man slaps me around the face with a wet tea towel for no reason. Within seconds I have one hand around his throat and I am punching him in the stomach with the other. By the time the police arrive he is vomiting on the floor. This time I'm given a different room at the Charing Cross Hotel.

Length of Stay:	1 night
Room Service:	Three cups of nice tea and a biscuit.
Bill:	A caution
Rating:	★★★★

The Transvestite Incident

I round up three Regulars, an Occasional and add two Paid-Fors to make up the numbers. One of the Regulars, Noleen, actually has a real job as a make-up artist. After a few lines and half-a-dozen bottles of champagne, this is what she suggests:

—Let's dress Lincoln up as a woman!

I think:

—That's a great idea.

We go back to my flat and take a dress one of the Wraps left in my wardrobe and a long, blonde wig Suzie keeps in my flat for when she's doing a shoot in the studios on Berwick Street. As Noleen puts the eyeliner and lipstick on, I actually begin to fancy myself. When I'm done, the Occasional offers to lend me her long coat and handbag and we leave for a party I've been invited to in the Marriott on Park Lane. We stop for an impromptu fashion shoot with the boys at The Office. In between shots I go to the toilets to pound and snort and, by the time we leave, another half dozen or so Wraps have joined us, together with Maynard, Steve and Daniel, the tailor.

When we arrive at the Marriott, I am in the grip of A Great Madness. I am Invincible and Murderous. The doorman at the Marriott takes a look at my wig and the lipstick, which is now smudged all over my face and issues his own Death Warrant:

—I'm sorry, sir, but I cannot let you into the hotel in your present condition.

I ignore him and barge into him. As he falls against the wall, three bouncers appear from nowhere. I swing at them and when I connect with one of them, my handbag breaks open and a Lady Finger vibrator, some make-up and a box of tampons fall to the ground. The Wraps are screaming and one of the boys is shouting:

—Lincoln! Lincoln! Stop! Stop! They'll kill you!

I can't stop. Ever.

By the time the police arrive I have taken two of the bouncers out and when I am carried, writhing and swearing, into the police van, I can hear a man pleading with them:

—Take it easy, she's a fucking woman.

When I get to my room at the Charing Cross Hotel, a few of the coppers take pictures of me on their mobile phones. One of them shouts:

—C'mon, Lincoln, give us a twirl.

I rush at the bars of my room and tell him to fuck off. He laughs:

—Time of the month, is it?

After maybe an hour, I start shaking and wrap my coat around my torn dress to keep warm. It's nearly midday when I wake up.

Length of Stay:	1 night
Room Service:	Two glasses of water and a fashion shoot.
Bill:	A caution
Rating:	★

The Stalking Incident
About midnight on a Wednesday evening I come out of the

Aqua Bar and walk down Great Marlborough Street with my friend Martin. I am hammered but my radar for potential violence is as strong as ever and I notice we're being followed by a gang of six or seven blokes. One of them shouts at me:

—Hey, baldy!

My first instinct is to kill them. My second is to ignore them because they are seven and we are two, and I'm not sure how useful Martin will be in a fight, so it might be one and a half, or even one. Then he shouts it a second time and I turn and run at them. Martin follows behind, but long before he gets anywhere near them I have laid two of them out and two others saw what I did and ran away. Now it's more even. To be fair, Martin has a go at one of them while I take on the other two. They catch me with a couple of blows but I know where to strike: the solar plexus and the side of the neck. When they're both down, I begin kicking hell out of them when three cops jump on me from behind. In the back of the car on the way to the Hotel, one of them says:

—Not many people could do what you just did. Then again, not many people would want to.

Length of Stay:	2 hours
Room Service:	Two glasses of water and one black coffee
Bill:	No charge
Rating:	★★★

The Battering Ram Incident

Drink. Coke. Some cunt in the toilets at The Office then a short walk to The Box, a nightclub set between sex shops and peep shows on an alley called Walker's Court. By an Act of

God I cannot understand I am on the Guest List. I walk up the stairs to the main floor area. Simon Hammerstein, the owner and grandson of Oscar Hammerstein, is sitting at a table surrounded by Wraps in sexy white dresses with tight little arses. My favourite things.

Terry is at the bar selling non-existent investment opportunities for the Cannes Film Festival to Georges, a Parisian hedge fund manager. They move to a booth. Perfect. I join them and nestle in the corner, snorting a few lines from a discreet little coke dispenser I bought in a sex shop on Broadwick Street. Esurio says:

—That was a good buy, Lincoln, very handy.

I take a moment to think how smart I am when I knock my vodka tonic over Georges's lap. I go to grab the glass as it falls on his crotch. I think I touch his cock. He thinks I touch his cock. I apologise. He accepts. With a smile. I don't like that smile, so I look away at the main floor of the club. The Box is *The Place to Be* in Soho and when a club becomes the *The Place to Be*, it has to deliver even more than its reputation, which means:

- More tits
- More cunt
- More madness

The show doesn't start well. A couple swallowing swords. No tits. No cunt. No madness. I take another line as the audience throw ice cubes at the couple. The girl runs off stage. The guy says fuck off and someone throws an ice bucket at him. Next on is a stunning-looking Wrap called Narcissister who strips then pulls a ringing mobile phone from her pussy.

The audience roars. Tits. Cunt. Madness. Esurio floats onto the stage, picks up the phone and throws it at me:

—Our time now, Lincoln, this is our time!

I pull a dozen Wraps off the dance floor into our booth. Champagne shoots in all directions, flooding the VIP booth next to us. My cock is being rubbed. I follow the arm to the face. Not Georges. A Wrap. My mind is playing a familiar mantra: Drink. Coke. Cunt. Drink. Coke. Cunt. I am the Beast of the Box and my nervous system is feeding off an ancient madness that flows through me like electrified water. On the stage a rapper shouts:

—Anyone want to hit this shit?

We all do and we are all One as we dance and shout, an anonymous tribe wasting ourselves as the rapper drums a gangsta beat from the stage. *My* stage! I crush some gear between two coins and sniff the holy powder and I am the King of Kings and the message I bring is Chaos. I run towards my stage. In the wings, Simon is naked and runs onstage before throwing himself at the mercy of the crowd. I follow him and am about to offer myself to the mass of bodies, *My* bodies, when I feel a punch land on my left ear and I begin to hear strange, pagan voices. And Esurio:

—That will hurt in the morning, Lincoln, very much!

I run across my stage, down some stairs and into a big, fucking kitchen.

There's a door in the far corner and I knock it off its hinges. I'm in a room with 'Buck Angel', one of the star acts, a muscle man with a cunt. For a moment I am in awe of the ingenuity of Nature, then I'm running again until two bouncers pull me to the ground and I'm hitting them with a traffic cone full of sand and, when it explodes, sand shoots into their eyes. Esurio says:

—You're in trouble now, Lincoln, Big Trouble.

I think:

—I'm in trouble now ... Big Trouble.

The bouncers get up and jump on me and one of them puts me in a headlock. I'm wriggling and squirming and shouting and kicking and spitting as three more bouncers join them on the stage. Together they carry me through the seated area down some stairs until we reach the main entrance. The door is shut and a security guard is about to open it when one of the men carrying me shouts at him to leave it shut, and they lower me to waist level and use my head as a battering ram. The impact hurts but I manage to force it open first time. They drop me in the alley outside and take a breather while I groan on the ground and call them cunts. I have no shirt, torn trousers, no watch, one shoe, a black eye, a throbbing head, no money. I feel the boot of a bouncer in my ribs and I can hear sirens in the distance and I know men in blue will take me from *The Place To Be* to the Charing Cross Hotel and when I get back to my flat my heart will pound and I will burn with anxiety and fear and be crushed with loneliness and the only defence I will have against a Darker Death is another drink, another line, another Wrap.

When I arrive at the Hotel I am beyond furious. I am in a Rage that is so intense it is off even my Scale of Fury. It takes five cops to get me into my room and I land at least four heavy blows on them as they do it. Once they get me in, they throw me on the floor and, as they leave, I rush up to the closing door and force my arm into the gap. They press the metal door against it until the pain is so great I can't take it anymore and I pull it in. I scream at one of the officers through the grill:

—Fuck you, you bald cunt! Come in here now!

Then I see four other officers approaching. One of them is wearing *The Glove*. This time I don't care. They can shove a diamond drill up my arse but they won't come out alive.

—Come on then, fucking try it!

I can't remember what happens next.

In the morning I am back in my flat. There are three Wraps in my bed. I do not know how I got here. I hear the sounds of Soho below me. I look up and the morning sun bursts on my half-opened eyes. I am blind and able to see the one thing I have left, draining away: Life.

Length of Stay:	1 night
Room Service:	1 mug of coffee and a visit from the Anal Inspector
Bill:	A caution
Rating:	★

The Paparazzi Incident

I come out of Bungalow 8 at about three in the morning with a celebrity Wrap when a Pap on a moped rides onto the pavement and catches me across the face with his camera as he passes. I push him off his bike and begin punching his head through his helmet. I hit him so hard I make a hole in the helmet and, as I'm about to put a dent in the side of his skull, three other Paps jump on me and begin kicking me. I manage to get free and take one of them out with a single punch. The other three start running up St Martin's Lane to get away from me. I rip my shirt off and chase them. I catch the straggler – a short, fat cunt – and bring him to the ground. I am beating the crap out of him and he knows his best hope is a deep coma, when two cops pile on top of me. I can hear one of them shouting breathlessly into his radio:

—It's Lincoln again; we're going to need some help.

In seconds they drag the Pap from underneath me and there are four, perhaps five, of them on top of me, forcing my face to the ground. Because of the angle I'm lying at, my ear is pressing so hard against the street I want to scream.

—Get off me! You're on my fucking ear!

The pain is unbearable and I think my head is going to explode. They don't release me until I'm cuffed and, when they do, the side of my face is numb and there's a huge gong crashing inside my head. When they get me to the Hotel, they leave me cuffed for a few hours and I fall into a deep sleep, my hands still bound when I wake up.

Length of Stay:	1 night
Room Service:	1 mug of coffee
Bill:	An assault charge
Rating:	★★

When I leave the Charing Cross Hotel after *The Paparazzi Incident*, I go back to the flat, take a shower and go for a run. I focus only on the rhythm of my feet as they pound the pavement. I go into a trance and, when I come round, I am two miles from Heathrow and my T-shirt is soaking with sweat. The run back is slower, more of a jog than a sprint, and when I get back to the flat I shower again and get changed. I am ready to go to The Office. During the run I was able to *Think About Things*. Here's what I thought:

- I can't remember the last time I smiled

- I don't want to smile ever again
- I am alive because of my fingernails
- Without them I would fall
- I am angrier than I have ever been
- I don't understand why I'm angry
- I don't care why I'm angry
- I love my son
- I need a drink
- I need a line
- I need a fuck

They may be fucked-up thoughts but they are my thoughts and they are honest. My Mum says:

—As long as you're honest in life, you won't go far wrong.

I think she would be proud I am her son. When I get to The Office, the boys and a few Wraps are waiting for me. Before I sit down, I go to the toilet and finish all the gear I have on me. The boys want to know everything, so I tell them everything.

I love telling stories. Telling is always better than Doing. When I Tell I am with other people, when I Do I am alone. When I Tell I am whoever they want me to be and it always feels better than Doing. I feel freer when I am Telling. I can run faster, fuck longer, punch harder and, in the world of Telling, I can be who I am without any consequences at all. I move through this world like an atom, undetected and unstoppable, being seen only when I choose and always in the best light. The world is made in the Telling and my words make it real. It ends only when I stop Telling and start Doing again, and then it goes all dark and troubled and I can't find my way around anymore until someone asks me what I have been Doing and the darkness breaks in the Telling of another story.

Before I leave The Office, I look in the mirror behind the bar and check if my handkerchief is sitting properly in my jacket pocket. It is perfect. I, however, am not. My skin looks taut and there is a quality in my eyes that seems new and ugly. Esurio says:

—That will be the Madness, Lincoln. Ripening so beautifully.

3 a.m.

I met Suzie in the Townhouse and we are in my flat. She is already naked. I am looking for my rope. Can't find it anywhere. I assume it's me that is absent and not the rope, so I look again. Under the bed, in the wardrobe, in the chest of drawers, in the kitchen cupboards, in the lounge. Nowhere. Suzie says:

—You get forgetful. It'll turn up.

I agree, but I have the suspicion I left it tied to the bedposts in a hotel somewhere in Soho. I look again in my chest of drawers and find a ball of blue car-towing rope. When I have her tied to the bed, she begs me to pound her and I pound her harder than I have ever pounded her before. She squeals and blows out her cheeks like a bellows to release the pressure from her head in case it explodes. She looks at me almost for the first time and sees the intense Fury that has taken me over in recent months. I have passed the point of insanity. I am made of Rage. The doorbell goes. I get off Suzie and go to the hall. It's the Paid-For we booked. I watch a dark-haired Wrap walk up the stairs in red stilettos. She looks at me and freezes, just for a second, but long enough for me to know that she can see it too. I tell her to go into the bedroom. My face is leaden like a statue or a corpse in the first stages of *rigor mortis*. She arcs around me and I follow in behind her. As soon as she sees Suzie, breathless and tied up with blue towing rope, she stops, turns around and runs out. She daren't look at me and is in such a hurry to get out of my flat, one of her red stilettos falls off and she hobbles down the stairs and back out into the comparative safety of middle-of-the-night Soho. I pick up the stiletto and take it with me into the bedroom. I will find uses for it.

1 a.m. The Next Day

My need to pound, to make ever deeper, more permanent marks on every Wrap I see, is marking my own face with madness. Because I only see myself from the inside, I consider myself to be charming and fun and wonder what the fuss is about when a Wrap looks at me as if I'm an extra from the set of *American Psycho*.

I have a Wrap with me in a taxi. We met in a club in Kensington where I had to meet a hedge fund manager who's bringing his sales team to The Club tomorrow night. I notice she is shifting in her seat. I have taken more than a week's worth of gear in one night. I ask her:

—Do you like porn?

—Yes I do.

I'm not convinced so, when we stop at some traffic lights, I put my hand on her thigh:

—I'm really gonna fuck you like you've never been fucked before.

The lights turn green and the taxi moves on and, as it does, the Wrap opens the door, jumps out in the middle of the junction and runs as fast as she can in the opposite direction. The driver catches my eye in the mirror:

—Whatever chat-up line you used there, mate, needs some more work before you use it again.

It's not the line. It's me. Something has changed. Not a total personality change, more of an *enhancement* of what has always been there.

When I was sixteen and shagging June, my Mum's mate, in the back of my Ford Fiesta, she used to say:

—There's something in you, Lincoln. It's a good thing but it's almost too much and, if you don't keep a careful eye on it, one day it will be a bad thing.

I guess that day has come. Here's more evidence:

- I have always been great with kids. The other day, one of the Grannies I've been seeing walked down Berwick Street with her grandchild. When we stopped to talk, the kid, who is about seven, hid behind her. When they walked on I heard him say:
  —He's a funny-looking man, Grandma.
- When I'm in the gym, familiar faces no longer greet me. If they can't avoid eye contact, they fake a smile and look down before I can speak to them.
- I have never cared less about my life, whether it goes on or stops.
- I have become a Fatalist. I believe there is nothing I

can do to change the direction of my life and I am happy about that.

- I have stopped mid-fuck three times in the last week because the Wrap asked me too.
- The fact that I am still able to stop is the only sliver of hope I have left.
- My dreams are terrifying and I often wake up screaming. These are the dreams I have had in the last week. They are typical of the dreams I have every week:

I'm running through a park full of trees and plants. As I run, the trees and plants all die around me and the sky goes dark. A squirrel comes up to me holding an acorn and tells me if I plant it, some new trees will grow and the park will be a nice place again. When I reach down to take the acorn, I see it is infested with maggots.

I am walking through a desert in the blazing heat. I know I will die unless I can find water. In the distance I see a woman walking towards me holding a baby's bottle. As we pass, she offers it to me. I take it but there's only a tiny bit of water in the bottom. I tell her it's not enough for both of us and she had better keep it. She tells me she has drunk enough to last her at least another day and tells me to drink. I put the rubber teat of the bottle to my mouth and drink and I notice there seems to be much more water in the bottle than there was when the woman gave it to me. When I go to take the bottle to see how this is possible, I can't get it out of my mouth. It's stuck in the upright position and the water keeps coming and coming and I know I'm going to drown in it.

I'm in The Club and all the Wraps are naked. I am naked too and my cock is hard, but every time I approach a Wrap and ask her to fuck me she just laughs until the noise of laughter is so great I run out of The Club to get away from it, but when I walk out into the street I find myself in a giant circus tent and I take a bow but there is no audience. An undertaker in a black suit walks up to me and asks me to step into a coffin. When I do, he closes the lid on top of me.

I'm in a room where there are no windows or doors and every inch is covered in exotic fabrics and curtains with Asian designs on them. I know there is no way out, so I just sink into the cushions and take in the smell of incense. I notice the silence is very deep but I wonder why I can't hear my own breath. I put my hand over my mouth. I can't feel my breath either, so I try to feel my pulse and again there is nothing but I feel so comfortable in this room, I close my eyes and fall asleep. This is the scariest of all my dreams. I have no idea why this is so.

The Secret Society

I have always found the best way to deal with the consequences of my own stupidity is do something even more
stupid.

The Boss has heard about the arrests and he wants to know
what the fuck is going on. I can't remember what I tell him
because I just want to get out of The Club and have a drink,
so I do my best to sound apologetic and hope he just lets me
go. He doesn't. He goes at me, so I say:

—Perhaps I'd better just fuck off then.

He says:

—Perhaps you better had. Mark will put the ten grand we
owe you into your account today.

And that's it. I'm finished at The Club. As I walk up the
stairs, I don't think about anything except where the next
drink is coming from. Esurio is waiting for me at the top and
opens the door onto Berwick Street:

—Bravo, Lincoln! Even by your standards, to relieve yourself of your only source of income, without any prospect of
replacing it, is commendable indeed.

—I'll replace it.

—How, if you don't mind me asking?

—I haven't had time to think about that yet.

—But you will.

—Of course.

I don't really care about my income because all I want is a drink, a line, a fuck, and my prefrontal cortex is in such a fragile state, not even Einstein could convince me of the connection between the capacity to think and a healthy bank balance. It's just gone ten when I get to The Office and everything is reassuringly normal. Maynard and Terry didn't make it home last night and slept on the floor behind the bar. They look unshaven and ridiculous. They greet me like the Prodigal Son. Like I said: reassuringly normal. As I get into the first vodka tonics of the day, I tell them I have resigned my job. They say:

—That was brave.

Then:

—And what are you going to do now?

To any normal person, this is a perfectly sensible question, but they only ask because they understand it's the proper thing to do. They don't even wait for an answer, which is fine by me because the only answer I have is another vodka tonic. At some point over the next few hours I make a quick calculation. I can't swear by its accuracy because at the time I do it, I am only able to count in multiples of a thousand, so the margin of error is significant. Here it is:

I have one bank account with Banco Santander because they are the only bank stupid enough to give me access to my own money. I am one thousand pounds in credit and I have a card from the same bank with an unused limit of two thousand pounds, plus the ten thousand coming from The Boss, which leaves me with thirteen grand. It seems a good number but it's meaningless to me, so I convert it into booze, gear and Wraps. That's when the panic sets in. I will be skint in less than a month. I try to think of a plan. I begin by listing in my head what I'm good at:

- Pounding
- Selling
- Drinking
- Snorting

Esurio suggests I flog tickets for *Public Pig Shagging* outside Vinopolis in Southwark. Free booze for the under-10s. I think it's not a bad idea, but I tell him it's not that type of snorting. I think making a list of *What Matters to Me Most* will help get my mind right. It's the same four items on the list. I have noticed of late that my range of interests has become more compressed. I listened as a kid to Patrick Moore telling me how big space was and how much stuff there was in it. How could he lie to a fucking kid? Space is bottle-sized and shrinking. Before long I will have the life squeezed out of me but not before I've solved *The Problem of How to Earn Money Next Month*.

The Problem of How to Earn Money Next Month
I don't know exactly when the idea came to me. Esurio tried to take the credit. He can have my soul but not this idea. This one belongs to me. In between bottles and lines, I remember that The Boss never took me up on the idea of running parties for some of The Club's Diamond Card Holders and calling them Secret Society parties. I think the idea of a Secret

Society of bankers and other robbers, who will pay me to get them Wraps in secret locations, sounds like my kind of business. I especially love the idea of it being a secret, so as soon as I have thought about it I tell everyone. Within a week I have somehow managed to get a website up and some business cards made. The website gives away no information, mainly because I haven't got a clue what I'm doing. At one point I think of changing the name from Secret Society to Lincoln's Drug Fund, to make it sound like some kind of offshore trust or specialist financial operation. Fortunately, I'm still a few lines short of accepting the merits of that idea when I settle once and for all on Secret Society.

Then I hit the phones. The first call is to Tina. I'm going to need at least fifty Wraps for every party and she can sort the booze out as well. The punters can bring their own fucking gear. It's all going well, when a Swedish bloke called Erik who drinks with us sometimes comes up to me in The Office and says:

—I hear you're going to be running a Secret Society and members will have access to parties with lots of birds in them.

I wonder how he heard about it. It's a secret. Then:

—Well, if you're interested I've got some connections with people who run beauty contests in Eastern Europe, Russia and Asia. If you want the winners to come over, they'll fly and fuck for ten grand each for three days. Including expenses.

Within ten minutes, I've done the deal, except I haven't got ten grand. I did have thirteen but that was nearly two weeks ago and it's down to five if I'm lucky. I need someone else's money. I call Rik:

—What? Real Beauty Queens? How many?

—I can get a maximum of five a time.

—How much?

—Get me ten members of the Secret Society at ten grand a shot plus five grand admission to every party.

—There's not enough Beauty Queens for that.

—Sure, but there's all the other girls. The best. You know you can trust me when it comes to girls.

—OK. Leave it with me.

I have that conversation with maybe a dozen different people. I forget how much money these guys have got. They got it from their customers, who have lost their homes by now, so Rik sees fit to take the price of their dreams and pass it on to me:

—And remember, Lincoln, I get first choice.

—Sure.

I have that conversation more times than I can remember and promise a decade's worth of Beauty Queens. I decide I will worry about the consequences of those conversations when I need to. So within a month I find myself in the improbable situation of having more thousands in my Banco Santander account than I am able to count. Even when sober. The only downside to this whole deal is that when people give you money, they all seem to want something for it, so I wish I had called it Lincoln's Drug Fund, then I could disappear and die in peace.

Tina sets up three parties for me: one in a big fucking townhouse in town, another on a boat on the Thames, then it's a fetish party out of town somewhere near High Wycombe. I check with her that the booze and the Wraps are all set up. I call the members of the Society and tell them the good news. They are all pissing themselves with excitement. A few of them have no class and ask me if they get any paperwork for being members and is it only three parties they get for their money? I threaten to give them their money back and let someone else have their place in the Society. I ask them:

—How can you have paperwork for a Secret Society?

They back off. With every cell in my brain stuffed full of gear, I can forget what day it is but I always remember how to sell. When I take one line too many and the fat lady sings, I know for sure she'll hire the venue from me. I even manage to create three Principles of the Secret Society.

PRINCIPLES OF THE SECRET SOCIETY

1. Membership is strictly limited
2. Breach of confidentiality will lead to immediate expulsion
3. Given the highly secretive and sensitive nature of the Society's parties, all payments are made at Members' risk

I even have a mission statement: *Put the promise of pussy before a man and he'll believe anything. Threaten to take it away and he'll pay anything.*

The first party is organised for a Thursday evening. I could have got five Beauty Queens in for the night but I've had to settle for three, mainly due to the diversion of Society funds up my nasal cavity. I tell Erik I want them in on Wednesday for 'testing'. When they arrive, they are the Crown Jewels of Wraps: two blondes, one brunette, with fake tits, shaved pussies and broken English. All I can think of when I see them is how to decide in which order to bang them.

The money was sorted before they boarded the plane. We

meet in my room at the Sanderson Hotel just after lunch and I say:

—OK. Who's first?

The Wraps look at each other. I lay out nine lines on the coffee table.

—Let's try again. Who's first?

Now, of course, they are all first. I notice I am enthusiastic. I actually *want* to fuck them and, when I am doing it, I don't want it to end. I solve the problem of order. I don't ask their names. I want places not names. It turns out they are the winning Wraps from Slovakia, Romania and Kazakhstan. I fuck them in geographical order from west to east. I'm not sure where Kazakhstan is but I guess it's the furthest east, so I make them all bend over and run a line from Slovakia through Romania to Kazakhstan. One line, hundreds of miles long. I pound with a rage I have never pounded before. To mark a Wrap is one thing. To mark the Crown Jewels of Wraps is a guarantee of immortality. When I'm finished, Slovakia can't walk, Romania is in pieces and Kazakhstan is on her knees trying to repair the bed.

The Next Night. The Night of the first Secret Society Party. 10 p.m.

The house is full of Wraps. I'm checking a few things with Tina.

—How many Asians and Eastern Europeans have you got?

—Shit loads.

—OK. Tell two of them they're Beauty Queens for the night.

—What? Real ones?

—Of course. I told the Members we've got five Beauty Queens coming over and I've only got three and one of those has been on it since yesterday in the Sanderson. So I need two more.

The Members start arriving at ten-thirty. When they walk in, there are thirty-two Wraps ready for action, a cocktail bar and eleven bedrooms, two beds in each. The Wraps are all wearing evening dresses. My idea. The only idea I had all day. By midnight, the house is heaving and the evening dresses have come off. Rik was first off the mark:

—Which ones are they, Lincoln?

I point out the Crown Jewels to him and he stares like he's just been let out of a monastery after ten years and stumbled into a brothel. Now that I've banged them, the Crown Jewels look no different from the other Wraps. In fact, some of the Russian Wraps Tina managed to get hold of are fucking stunning, but the judgement of the eye is a slave to opportunity. I look again and this time I do my best to believe they are the Jewels I believed them to be when I first saw them. No change. I am looking out at a sea of Wraps and one Wrap blends seamlessly into another, as wave after wave of monotony washes over me.

Tina brings two Asian Wraps over to meet Rik. They introduce themselves as Bangkok and Vietnam. When Rik wanders off with them, I turn to her:

—You could at least have let him have the real ones.

—They're already taken and, anyway, you said they were all real. Remember?

She's right. There's no difference between a real Crown Jewel and a fake one. What matters is that you *believe* there is a difference, and Rik, like all men, is a believer. I'll tell him one day he got the fakes and his memory will turn sour. But for now I'll leave him alone in his fantasy because what he believes he's doing matters so much more than what he's actually doing.

As the night goes on I get my cock sucked a few times by some Eastern European Wraps who always seems to put more effort in than English Wraps. The Boss said to me once:

—No points for effort, only results.

I think he got that one wrong. When I have some Bulgarian Wrap eating my cock like her life depends on it, effort is price-less. We had rules at The Club. The Wraps had to work at least every other weekend. Unless there were *exceptional circumstances*. Here's an exceptional circumstance:

I was in The Club at about four in the morning when this Croatian Wrap was arguing with George. It ended with her saying:

—Look, I'm not working again this week or next weekend. That's the way it is. You see the people who pick me up, you don't want to mess with them. So I am telling you I'm not working and I suggest you agree with me.

He did, and she waved at him from the blacked-out S-Class that picked her up twenty minutes later.

If you take your clothes off for a living, effort and hardship go hand-in-hand. You can't expect a Wrap from Romford whose ambition in life is to graduate to a sky-blue G-string and a bigger mojito, to put in the same effort as a Wrap who arrives at the club from a war zone. Einstein called it relativ-ity. I call it common sense.

As the night goes on, the bankers are cashing in their investment. At ten grand a shot, including membership, this is costing them one sub-prime repossession each, and they always want value for money. I catch a glimpse of Trevor in a corner with a Wrap on each arm. He's in his late-fifties, maybe sixty, proud of his own hair and greedy with one of those leering faces that looks up at you and saps your energy like a sponge. I wonder how the fuck he made it to the board of one of the big banks. Perhaps he drained the life out of the competition. I smile. He smiles back. Somewhere he's got a wife waiting for him who thinks he's meeting international clients. I wonder what it would be like if men like him were honest:

—Hi, darling, I'm home. Just fucked two girls and I'm much more hopeful about us than I was before I had my cock sucked.

If only, for one brief moment, married men could be honest without having to face the consequences. I never understood why women value honesty in men when, if we spit out the truth for a nano-second, we're cast aside like the plague. Perhaps we're better at statistics than women, which is why we have a good grasp of this issue. Here's some *Very Sad Numbers*:

- Married men get fucked 68.5 times a year by their wives
- 20% of married men get fucked less than ten times a year (A YEAR!!!) by their wives
- 50% of married women have little or no interest in sex

This is the reason why Good Men have Big Secrets and those secrets are made at a party like this. All that has to happen to make it right is for men to be honest, women to get a grip on the *Very Sad Numbers*, and do something about it. Except women *are* doing something about it. Here's some *Very Happy Numbers*:

- 80% of married British women have had at least one affair
- 64% of American women have had at least one affair

So Good Men go out, get fucked, go home and live another lie while their wives are out shagging men like me. The issue for married women is never sex. It's husbands. Get rid of them and the sex comes rolling back like a tsunami. I know because I drown in it. And the real difference between the sexes? Women are just more subtle hypocrites.

Someone grabs me from behind. When I turn to deck him, I see it's Rik and manage to stop myself an inch from his face.

—Fucking hell, Rik, I could have killed you.

—*You* kill *me*. What about the Crown fucking Jewels girls? You told me they were real and mine are made by Gerald fucking Ratner!

—Not exactly fakes, Rik ...

—Not exactly fakes?! Bangkok is a waitress from a fast food restaurant who's here in the hope of finding a cock with a wallet big enough to pay her college fees because there's too many chicken drumsticks to the pound, and Vietnam says she'd like to be a model one day, perhaps when she's a bit older. What the fuck is she waiting for? Asian Grannies?

I like the sound of that, but do my best to disguise it.

—OK, Rik, but did you have a good time?

—I was having a good time until I found out the truth. I

know this is a Secret fucking Society but not telling me who
the real Crown Jewels are is one secret too many.

I call Tina over. She can barely walk and has white powder
on her cheeks. I start explaining the situation and give up
when she falls over. I grab Rik by the arm and pull him after
me. We go through room after room of people fucking, drinking, snorting, and in about the fourth bedroom we go into I
see Romania taking a line. She's a monument to endurance.
She's been stuffing gear up her nose all day and still looks
fresh enough to keep a bloke attached to his right hand long
enough for his cock and hand to fuse together.

—Rik, this is Romania. Romania, this is Rik.

He puts his hand on her waist and leans into her so she can
hear him above the music.

—Are you real?

—Excuse me?

—Are you a real Beauty Queen?

She pulls away from him, scrolls through her iPhone and
shows him a picture. He smiles. As I walk out of the room, I
feel a shooting pain in my arm. At first I think I'm going to
have a heart attack. It's long overdue, so it might as well
happen here. I keep walking, expecting to drop at any
moment, when the pain passes and I am left with a familiar
feeling of Nothing. Fuck all. It washes over me like a tsunami.

I used to dream of running parties with Crown Jewels and
having my own name up in lights:

Lincoln Townley: The Great Impresario.

Lincoln Townley: The Best Gentlemen's Parties in the World.

Lincoln Townley: The Sexiest Shows in Town.

But dream and reality rarely meet. Naked Wraps, champagne, cocaine, a sea of writhing, falling, shooting bodies, and

I couldn't give a fuck. I might as well be wandering through a desert.

The next day I get a call from Nick, who takes so much coke I never understand how he manages to get to the stock market never mind trade in it.

—That was amazing, Lincoln. When's the next one?

—Two weeks. On a boat.

—Great. But don't go taking on any more members. Secrets are best shared between as few people as possible.

—Yeah, right.

I think:

—Is he really that fucking stupid?

He's just paid more than he ever should for a party with Wraps he could get any night of the week but, because I put 'Secret' in the title, he thinks it's something special. OK, the Crown Jewels were a bit special, but there were only three of them and he probably never got near any of them.

I go online and look at my bank account. It seems to have money in it so I assume I have accidentally hacked someone else's account. I look at the screen and it definitely has my name on the top. I wonder where all the money has come from. After expenses, I appear to have over thirty grand. That's what one single, grubby little word can do. Put 'secret' before whatever it is you're doing and you've put a zero on the price. These guys can get whatever they want whenever they want it. Booze. Gear. Wraps. More than they can ever take. But there's one thing they can never get enough of and that's the fact that they get things other men can't. I think it might be a good idea to close the membership book, charge more and offer less for the next party. I call it cheating. They call it status.

*

The Secret Society looks like it has a future. Then it all goes to shit. Here's what happens:

- The second party, I call it *Secrets on the Thames*, is going well until some cunt lets off a flare and the skipper takes the boat back to harbour.
- The next day I get over fifty calls giving me a hard time. I say:
  —It wasn't me who let off the flare.
  They say:
  —But you're the founder of the Society and we want a refund or a free party.

I feel like telling them there is no fucking Society. It's something I dreamed up when I took too many drugs and lost my job and it's the only way I could pay my bills. It's not fucking real. Then they'll say:
  —Well, it feels real to us. The women are real. The booze is real. The gear is real. And we are Members and you can't be a Member of Nothing. Especially if you've paid for it.

- I look at my bank account and this time I know it's mine because it's fucking empty.
- Somehow I manage to get it together to stage the third and what turns out to be final Secret Society Party, *The Mad Masquerade*. I don't quite have the funds to hire a country house, so we make do with an empty warehouse. There are a few complaints but I tell them it's never been used for a private party before and it's only because the Society is so exclusive that the owner was proud to let me have it. Amazingly, the Members believe me. The truth

is, it's used for sex shows, but they're off air for one night and I promised Tim, who owns it, a Crown Jewel if he let me have it and we split the bar. All good except I don't have any Crown Jewels coming to this one. I decide to worry about that later.

- The party goes well but the Members are getting restless. These are some of the questions I am asked:

    —Can we have a Membership card? I know it's all secret but a card would be nice.

    —The parties are great, Lincoln, but when are we doing to take them to the next level. You know what it's like; we've done this, *three times*, so what's next?

    —Have you thought about giving Members additional]benefits? Perhaps a concierge service or a party in Monaco?

Of course I haven't thought about it. I haven't thought about anything except how I'm going to get enough cash for next bottle of Rioja, the twenty shots a day I need to survive, and the Mount Everest of Cocaine I need to get me through the day.

I realise I'm a bit stuck. I have no money, and the chances of Members getting another party are more likely if Elvis was organising it. So I close the Society down. I email every Member and tell them the bad news while being careful to remind them of the Third Principle of the Society that 'all payments are made at Members' risk'. Most of the Members seem to accept it. They've had three great parties but, much more than that, they've had three great parties *other men couldn't get access to.* One or two complain but they soon disappear when I suggest that perhaps they overstretched themselves when they became Members, and that if they can't see the value in having unrestricted access to London's most beautiful women, then in future they should stick to weddings and bar mitzvahs.

When the last Members are off my back, Esurio asks me:

—So what have you learned, Lincoln?

—That I don't want to do parties anymore.

—And . . .

—I'm a great salesman. The best.

—And . . .

—I'm lost.

—Anything else?

—I don't really want to do anything. Fuck all.

Losing My Mind

Since the last Secret Society party I have been wondering if it's possible to crack up and not know it. Or to crack up and know it only after it's happened. Like a delayed reaction. With me it happened in four stages:

The First Stage
When I told Esurio I didn't want to do anything, I didn't think I meant it. I just said it. The truth was I still felt there must be something out there I want to do. It was a matter of finding it. Even if it was fishing or stamp collecting. There *had* to be something. I think it was the Geek with Glasses who said that if there is something meaningful to find, you will find it when you need it most.

He was wrong. There was nothing. Absolutely fuck all.

I decided to lose myself in a good book and got as far as staring blankly at the fiction shelves in Waterstones on Piccadilly before walking out empty-handed. The next day I took a trip over to the Tate Modern to see the Gauguin exhibition. After sitting before a naked woman and a South Sea island for half an hour, I moved only when one of the curators woke me up with a gentle tap on the shoulder. The single useful purpose the painting served was to remind me I was in a gallery where it is not appropriate to punch him in the face for touching me.

Even when I'm running or working out in the gym, my mind is empty. One foot goes out before the other and I lift weights as heavy and pointless as they have ever been. Without any enthusiasm. I try banging the best-looking Wraps I can find and they muster a hard-on and a thimble of semen but, when I am at it, all I think of is tiling my Mum's kitchen floor or standing by dark pools of water counting the ripples. My last hope is the booze and the gear. Night after night I get to the 'red zone' as fast as I can and wait for the euphoria, the ecstasy of drunken anticipation, to wash over me and carry me from one Technicolor adventure to the next. Nothing happens. Worse than nothing. I realise getting hammered has become a habit as dull and relentless as a grey, February sky. I begin to panic so, one night, I say to Maynard:

—What matters to you?

—Bit early for that Linc, isn't it?

—No, seriously, what matters to you?

—Um ... I don't know ... I'd have to think about it ...

A Terrible Thought grabs hold of me. Perhaps I have become another *Lost Man of Soho*, not even looking for a way out, just hunting for a broken compass to help me pretend, for a few useless moments, that having a way out or not having a way out makes a difference.

The Second Stage
This happens when I know that I really don't want to do anything. This 'knowing' isn't something open to debate. It is a matter of absolute certainty, the kind of certainty that wakes

me up in the middle of the night and leaves me gasping for air. It is a necessary prelude to the second stage of my crack-up: Isolation. This is when I reach the end of whatever ridiculous journey I am making and wait for someone to greet me only to learn there is no one there. I am totally alone. There never was anybody there. There never will be anyone there.

When Dad died, I remember how he looked, lying on the gravelled ground of a caravan park with only a stranger beating at his chest and a spooky see-through man in a long coat and bowler hat for company. It freaked me out when I thought about it. I used to think that what got to me was the fact that he was dead but now I am a *Lost Man of Soho*, what gets to me is that he died alone. That we all die alone. Life after death happens to the living not the dead. It begins the moment we realise how cut off we are from other people.

My life has become a daily grind of crushing loneliness. I laugh and drink with the boys at The Office, pound the Wraps, chat to barmen and shopkeepers, without ever feeling I am *with* them. There is no bridge between my world and theirs. Perhaps there never was and, even if such a bridge once existed, the ropes have been cut. All that's left is the rush of air past my ears as I wait for my body to hit the ground and lie undiscovered for centuries.

There's a homeless man who sleeps on Poland Street and begs around Soho. I see him often when I come out of The King's Arms and he is always alone. I see him one afternoon on Dean Street. I buy his attention with a quid and ask:

—Do you ever have any mates you knock about with? You know, just some company?

He has no answer because the question makes no sense to him. When loneliness gets into the soles of your shoes and the fabric of your shirt, 'company' has no meaning. Words that hint at connection are the language of the living. He, like me, no longer speaks it. The only consolation I have is that wherever I am, Esurio is always with me. I need him and the more he bullies me the more I need him. He is all I have left and, the closer I draw towards him, the lonelier I feel, so I draw even closer and he pulls further away, teasing me. I don't love him. I *crave* him. I know he loves me only because I am good sport, in the way a spotty teenager loves the pet cat he can trap on a swivel chair and spin around then throw it on the floor and watch it bump into the furniture and then do it again and again until the cat is sick and becomes epileptic and froths at the mouth and . . .

The Third Stage
After isolation comes fear.

I think it's the Thursday after the last party and I'm leaving a tapas bar on D'Arblay Street when I don't just feel alone. I am *aware* that I am alone. I am shining a light down a long narrow tube and looking at myself walking around Soho. Walking from one bar to another. Talking only to myself. There is never a person on the other side of the conversation. I speak and no one responds. When I hold my hand out, there is no one there to receive it. It is in this moment, moving like an ant in a desert, that I feel the horror of my situation and panic sets in. My hands and face are covered in sweat and my stomach is churning like a tumble-dryer. Without anyone to act as my mirror, to reflect back evidence of life, I do not have any proof that I exist, and fear squeezes me until I can't breathe. Without anything to hold me together, fear breaks me apart and I scatter around the streets of Soho like litter.

Fear has many faces. It's kind when it protects you from harm and warns you when you're in danger; when it tells you to move away from the shadows or forces you to look away from the smiling psychopath who offers to share your burden over a quiet drink. Fear is generous when it walks alongside you, pushing you past every gnawing thought of failure towards your greatest triumph. But then there is a Darker Fear. This is the Fear that consumes you. The Fear that worms inside your head and eats away at you until there is nothing left.

I have known all these fears but only one remains. The Darker Fear. When fear turns dark, it is never pure blackness. If it was all black, it might be bearable in the way that death is bearable, because it leaves you without any awareness of what has happened to you. Death is laced with *compassion*. But my Darker Fear is speckled with light, small fires of life, that let me know I am alive and in pain without any possibility of mercy. It flickers like the sparks a bound victim sees rising from the torturer's coals, as he lies semi-conscious, burning with pain, waiting for the touch of molten metal on his skin.

I turn into Wardour Street and I'm shaking. I need a drink and a line but I know they will not be enough to steady my nerves. The Darker Fear has consumed me and, as I turn right towards Dean Street, I know what has happened . . .

The Fourth Stage
. . . I have cracked up and now, perhaps some time after the event took place, I know I have lost my mind – without hope of finding it again. I imagine trawling the gutters of Soho in search of it and finding it lodged in a drain where I snatch it and clean it up and get it working again, but it is too late for that.

I have cracked up. I *know* I have cracked up. And I have just enough knowledge to feel the pain and see the hopelessness of my situation. Esurio can't stop gloating and hassling me. He has changed. He is colder, less easily satisfied, always demanding more of me and he changes shape. Sometimes he is his normal self, standing in a bar or blowing on a pussy, dressed in his black coat and bowler hat, his fingers bulging with fabulous rings made from amber and amethyst, spinning his cane on the end of his tongue, but other times he looks different, like he's some kind of shape-shifter.

I'm walking down Brewer Street and I can't see him anywhere but his voice is banging away in my head:

—Feed me, Lincoln, feed me.

—What do you want from me?

—Nourishment, all the nourishment in the world.

—I don't have anything left to give.

—Then find something to give, find it now!

We bicker all the way to The Office and when I sit down at my usual table at the back, Maynard follows in behind me. He looks like the doctor has just given him a diagnosis of terminal cancer, so I ask him:

—Are you OK, Maynard?

He pauses and says:

—I'm fine, Linc, but I'm worried.

—About what?

—About you.

I look at him. He goes on:

—I was behind you on Brewer Street and you were talking to yourself.

—I was just hearing him in my head.

—Who?

—Esurio.

—Who the fuck is Esurio?

—You must have seen him around. I hang out with him a lot.

Maynard is staring at me like he believes I should be in a padded cell.

—I'm just worried about you, talking to yourself and making up friends and it's not just me who thinks it ...

—Who else?

—All of us. I told the boys I wouldn't say anything but we all think you might be ... losing it a bit ...

I can hear Esurio roaring with laughter inside my head. I bang my head with my hands. Maynard shuffles away from me. The one thing worse than seeing your friend lose his mind is for him to lose it when you're sitting at the same table. I walk out onto Dean Street without saying anything.

It isn't just in the way he projects his voice that Esurio has changed. He seems to love changing his shape. There was the wild dog in the Charing Cross Hotel but that's not the only time he's changed. He's done it four times since the last Secret Society party:

The First Time

I'm walking along Greek Street when something catches my eye on the wall of a restaurant. I take a closer look and see that it's a lizard. I am about to turn away when it says:

—Don't you recognise me, Lincoln?

The voice is his. I tell him to fuck off. He doesn't like it:

—The problem with words, Lincoln, is they have consequences ...

He propels himself off the wall and lands on my face. I'm

tearing at him and trying to protect my eyes when I can feel blood on my fingers. His or mine? I can't be sure.

This attack is one of the things Maynard mentions to me when he gets concerned:

—And another thing. Simon saw you talking to a brick wall on Greek Street and then you were pulling at your face and screaming on the ground.

—Why didn't he come and fucking help?

Maynard looks down into his beer and shrugs his shoulders.

The Second Time

I'm having a wank in my flat looking at some Granny Porn where this filthy sixty-year-old is taking one up the arse from a young bloke when he turns into this goblin-like creature whose claws push out of the screen. I see his long nails are covered in a white powder and I snort it all and then my mind gets full of colours and I puke everywhere. When I wake up, probably a few hours later, I am lying in my own vomit and the goblin is standing over me:

—And not even a gesture of gratitude on your part. Pathetic!

I see him about to pounce on me then I go unconscious again.

The Third Time

I wake up and I stare at the ceiling. I can see it's mainly black with only the odd patch of white breaking through here and there. I'm about to get up when the black bits move. I strain my eyes to see what's happening and they seem to be falling towards me and in seconds my body is crawling with spiders, hundreds of them getting everywhere, in my arse, my mouth. I'm choking and flailing about in my room, bashing the walls, and I manage to get to the door and run out onto Old Compton Street, where Esurio covers me with a blanket and tells me to go back inside. I don't want to go. I am Fucking Terrified, but he guides me up the stairs and when I get back into my room the spiders are gone. He laughs and leaves me shivering under the covers.

The Fourth Time

I'm lying on my bed in the flat when a snake slithers between a gap in the door, crawls up onto the bed and rests on my stomach. It has skin made of black velvet and whispers to me:

—This time there is no way back. You know that don't you, Lincoln?

—Yes.

—Sorry, I didn't hear you ...

He prods me with his tongue, catching a nerve in my back.

—Yes, yes.

—We have had such a journey, you and I, but we are reaching the end now. Have you thought, Lincoln, how you want it to end?

—I don't care ... I don't care ...

—Now, there's no need to descend into indifference. Use your imagination. How about an overdose in the disabled toilets in The Office and you can lie there for perhaps an hour before Maynard goes for a pee and finds you? Or perhaps you can get into a fight in Ronnie Scott's. I know you're very fond of Ronnie Scott's, but this time your general malaise deprives you of that necessary timing; you just don't *care* enough to win, and you take a fatal blow to the side of the head. I can even arrange for you to have a grieving lady kneeling over your body ... No, that would be too sentimental and, quite frankly, you don't deserve it. I know! You can end it by your own hand. How about tying that blue car-towing rope you have in your flat to your bedroom door, wrap it around your neck, stand on a chair then push the chair away?

—I told you, I couldn't give a fuck ...

—Then I have an even better plan. Have you ever heard of the ichneumon wasp, Lincoln?

—Of course I fucking haven't.

—Well, it caused quite a scandal in the nineteenth century when such cruelty was beyond the imagination of a humble parish priest.

—What the fuck are you talking about?

—You see, the female ichneumon wasp injects her eggs into the body of a host, usually a larva, and as the larva develops, the eggs of the wasp hatch inside its body and when the larva is mature enough to provide a decent meal, the wasp slowly eats it from the inside, keeping its brain and nervous system alive long enough to make a feast of the organs. Then, when the larva is dead, the wasp just flies away. You hear that, Lincoln, it just flies away in search of its next meal.

—So you're saying ...

—... that you just allow yourself to be eaten alive.

—By whom?

—Do you really have to ask?

The snake hisses at me before gliding off the bed and out of my flat.

*

I'm drinking, snorting and pounding more than ever and I'm doing it to bring it all to an end, one way or the other. Esurio is with me all the way:

—It's your life, Lincoln. You can waste it any way you want.

When I was a teenager and Lewis was born I had nothing. We lived for a while in a hostel and made nappies out of bits of cloth, but at least I knew *why* I was there: I was preparing myself for a better life. One day the cloth would be a grand, velvet curtain and I would step out onto some enormous fucking stage: *The One, The Only, The Incomparable, The Magnificent, Lincoln Maximilian Townley*, and I am puking on Frith Street one night, and there's blood in my vomit, when I hear the compère calling inside Ronnie Scott's, blasting out the same words: *The One, The Only, The Incomparable, The Magnificent, Lincoln Maximilian Townley*. I walk up the narrow stairs into the club, wiping bits of lunch off my jacket, and when I get to where the voice is coming from, I see a stage and a microphone. I hear applause in my head and I think:

—This is it! All the waiting and now, when there's nothing left, it comes . . .

I climb onto the stage and begin singing. The noise from the crowd is so loud I can't hear myself think, and my head is hurting from the brightness of the lights and then I fall. I think I must have missed the end of the stage but someone catches me and carries me out of the club. When I'm back on Frith Street I take a line out of my pocket and Maynard passes me a bottle of beer:

—What the fuck are you doing, Linc?

—What do you mean? I just went on stage.

—I know you went on stage, but you took the mic off some Cuban band and began shouting nonsense.

—But it was my time, Maynard.

—Linc, you need help.

The last thing I need is help. How the fuck does he think anyone can reach me now? My head is broken into tiny pieces with bits spread out all over Soho. Someone might pick up a piece on Dean Street and shout, *I've got a bad thought*, and someone else will shout from Beak Street, *And I've got a bad feeling*, until there are hundreds of people, each one of them looking at a piece but not one of them has a picture that tells them where the pieces fit, so they throw them away and they get shuffled and reshuffled so many times that some of the pieces get lost and broken and then I know I am safe. I am irredeemably insane and no one can get near me. I cannot be reached by anyone.

I think it might help if I go to The Club for a few dances. I don't work there anymore, so no one can say anything. I cut across from Frith Street into Greek Street and make my way to Wardour Street. Outside The Club, Chris is on the door. He looks at me, looks at the ground, then looks up at me again, like he's preparing himself. The last time I saw him was just before I left The Club, when we sponsored him in an amateur boxing tournament.

—How are you doing, man?

—Good thanks, Lincoln.

I fluff up my handkerchief and notice it is wet with puke.

—I'm just coming to see some of the girls.

—Sorry, Linc, I can't let you in.

—What do you mean, you can't let me in?

—What I say. I can't let you in.

I go to push past him. He blocks my path. I want to kill him. I look him in the eye and, in that moment, his life or mine is saved because in a flicker of recognition he nods and lets me in.

—Make it quick, Linc. It's my head on the block.

—That's nothing, man, mine's already rolling.

I walk past the bar and leopard-skin seats and make my way downstairs to the main stage. I sit at a table in the front. There are three Wraps dancing. I recognise two of them. I watch them curl around the poles. I feel empty. I go to the toilet and take a line. When I come back I feel the same. I ask a blonde Wrap for a dance. We go to a booth and, before she has finished, I'm back on Wardour Street and I don't know where I'm going but I just keep on walking and, as I walk, I know there is only one person in the world I truly love, one person I want to share my life with, the one who has stood by me through all I have been through, who has been with me through all the highs and the lows and who will be with me when everyone else has gone. I look up at the sky and think how lucky I am to be able to love. To give and receive what matters most in life. A gift in return for a gift. And I know I am fortunate to have such love in my life when so many people live and die without ever feeling what I feel right now. I raise the bottle of beer I have in my hand and shout at the stars:

—Thank you, Esurio, thank you.

A Bigger Splash

November 2010. 3 a.m.

I'm sprinting down Brewer Street. I cut across Regent Street
and carry on down Conduit Street. I don't how long I have
been running or how long it will be before I collapse. Esurio
is right: I hadn't thought how I want it to end and now I know
it *has* to end, I *want* it to end, I want to die running. I feel the
pain in my chest getting more intense. I increase my speed. I
am struggling for breath. Sweat is rolling off my body like a
river. I feel consciousness ebb and flow and all the lights of the
city merge to create a vast ocean into which I know I am
falling. My heart is raging like a wild beast, eating me from the
inside out. I want to be free, to shatter the bones of my ribcage
and hurl my guts at the city walls. There are pauses in the
thud of my feet on the pavement. I know I am reaching the
end. I hear a siren wailing. I black out.

5 a.m.

I wake up on Albemarle Street, slumped in the doorway of the
Time & Space cafe. I move my feet and arms. They work. I

roll my head in circles and grab a ridge in the wall to help me to my feet. My heart is quiet. Content. I have learnt the difference between exhaustion and death. The one inevitably precedes the other but at a time of its own choosing. I know that time will come. It *has* to come. Just not yet.

6 a.m.

I shower and get changed in my bedroom. Knowing I am a husk, my life force cored out, is comforting. I have nothing left to lose. All I'm doing is waiting for my heart to stop beating and my body to reach the cracked-up state of my soul. I go online in search of one last Granny.

11 a.m.

I wipe my hand across my mouth, snuffle the last grains of cocaine from the hairs on my nose and make my way up a narrow staircase on Broadwick Street. I knock on a door and a woman in her early sixties answers.

—Brenda?

—Yes. Lincoln?

—Yeah.

She looks exactly like her picture on *Adult Friend Finder*. Her profile said: *Older woman looking for naughty domination*. I am loaded with Kamagra and need the kind of filth that only a Granny can give me. I need to pound her like she has never been pounded before, to leave a mark so deep, her grandchildren will ask:

—Grandma, what's **that** funny shape on your head?

It starts well. She leaves the room and comes back in a few minutes holding a whip and some handcuffs. She puts them on my hands and begins to bang me. She calls me a 'piece of shit', a 'pathetic wanker', a 'useless slave', and all the while she is whipping me and spitting on me and pinning me down. I struggle to free my hands and reverse the roles but the cuffs are metal and locked. I try telling her this is not how it is meant to be. I want to say:

—You've got this all wrong. Don't you know who I am?

But I am trapped and at her mercy. After maybe ten minutes of being assaulted, my cock collapses. Not all the Kamagra in the world could raise it from the ashes. She looks shocked and tries to resurrect it for a few minutes before surrendering. She releases me and says:

—It's all right, darling.

I hate the tone of her voice. I am her damaged child and she pets me like I'm a plaything of the Salvation Army.

When I'm back on Broadwick Street, Esurio can't resist:

—Well, that was a disaster, Lincoln.

—Fuck off.

—You know you're losing it, don't you? I wonder why I spent so much time nurturing you when all you do is disappoint me.

His voice rasps like a threshing machine:

—Do not let me down, Lincoln. Do not *dare* to let me down.

12:30 p.m.

I twist my face and lift a hundred kilograms above my head. The gym is full of noise but my head is quiet, focused like a bullet. I haven't eaten and I feel sick. My chest hurts. The gym fades in and out of my awareness. I have never felt so connected to my breath. I feel it rise and fall and, all the while, I am waiting for it to stop. I make my way to the pool. I stand on the edge and dive in. I open my mouth and feel my lungs fill with water. The pain in my chest grows more intense. I thrash about before I let go. The speckled light dancing through the water is the most beautiful light I have ever seen and everything is slowing down. I feel myself falling deeper when strong arms wrap themselves around my waist and carry me upwards. When my head breaks through the surface I gasp for air. My chest rattles with noise and pain. I look to see who it was carried me to the surface. There is no one there.

3 p.m.

I'm in my flat. I've turned the wall behind my bed into a canvas. My Granddad loved Hockney and I've painted *A Bigger Splash* dozens of times but this is largest copy I've ever done. I've pushed the bed towards the door and I have to stand on a chair to paint the skyline. My hand is moving across the wall at such a speed it feels like I'm not in control of it. I am lost in colour and movement.

When I'm done I stare at the landscape. It's complete except for the splash. The surface of the water is calm. It is still and brittle like glass. What if nothing *ever* disturbs it? What if the chaos of the splash never happens, if the trees and the water and the buildings are allowed to stay empty and dead? What if we never know there's someone under the water and we never have to follow him in?

I don't want to finish the painting. I can't. The painting is like a dam, holding back a torrent of fear, and I know if I finish it, if I paint the violence of the splash, I will drown in that fear. I think:

I'll make the biggest fucking splash anyone has ever made and then sink without trace.

I feel sick. I want to puke and shit. My body begins to tremble and my head starts spinning. I pass out and collapse on the floor. As I lie unconscious, I dream I float into the painting on the wall and this is what happens:

I feel the heat of the sun on my face and all I can see as I look up is clear blue sky. No clouds as far as my eye can see. A yellow diving board juts out over the pool. There is not a sound. Everything is dead. Across the pool are two tall palm trees towering over a single-storey building. The leaves of the trees are perfectly still, like they are made of stone. The building is long with a brown wall nearest the palm trees and large glass windows stretching floor to ceiling. There's an outline of another building in the glass and some grass growing against the wall. Nothing moves. In front of the windows is a chair, the kind you see on a film set, and an empty, monotonous patio area stretches out towards the pool. I move away from the yellow diving board. My feet are burning on the hot ground. I look out at the water. The surface is still unbroken, laid out before me like a sheet of glass. There is no splash. There is nothing under the water.

I look across at the long windows and something moves.

A shadow. Too fast for me to make out what it is. Then it is gone and I hear an enormous splash. It cuts the silence like a volcano. In the middle of the pool, water spews upwards. The diving board is still, not even the faintest of vibrations disturbs it, as if no one has even stepped on it, let alone jumped off it. My guts are gripped with fear. I follow whoever or whatever has jumped into the water. It feels like I'm underwater a long time before I see a shape a few yards away from me. At first, all I can see is a vague thrashing movement. As I get closer I see two bodies, one bigger than the other. A man and a boy. The man has his arms around the boy and he is leaning back. The boy's face is full of fear and confusion. As I get closer to them, the man lets go of the boy and swims up towards the surface. I shudder, as a black shape swims past me and I reach out to the boy. His body is still now, his head moving like a reed in the water. His body hits the bottom of the pool and he lies face down. Dead.

I swim to get closer to him but, before I reach him, I struggle for breath and push myself out to the surface. When I get there I let out a scream. As my eyes get used to the light, I make out the man I saw in the water. He is sitting on the director's chair by the single-storey building, smoking a cigar and wearing a white, frilled shirt, dark trousers and black boots with golden soles. His coat is wrapped around the back of the chair and there is a cane leaning against the side. Esurio.

I swim to his side of the pool and pull myself up onto the patio. I sit facing away from him, hunched, exhausted. I can't speak. Or move. As I sit by the water, I see a shape rising towards the surface. It breaks through close to where I am sitting. It's the boy, his face buried in the water. I reach out and pull him towards me. He looks big enough to be about thirteen. I turn him over to see his face and as I do, my guts convulse and I retch into the water.

—Recognise him, Lincoln?

I hold the boy's face in my hands. *My* face. *I* am the boy he took to the bottom of the pool.

—So, Lincoln, now you know who's under the water. Quite a splash, don't you think?

I let the boy go and watch as he sinks again under the water. When the boy is out of sight I get up to face Esurio. I want to kill him. I run at the chair and take a swing at him. My fists pass through his body as if he isn't there. He keeps smiling and staring at me and, with every pointless punch, I feel my strength drain away until I slump to the ground.

—He's a child, Esurio. How could you kill a child?

—What makes you think I killed him?

—I saw you, you cunt. I saw you take him to the bottom of the pool. He was struggling and you wouldn't let him go. You wouldn't let *me* go.

—It may have seemed that way, but I assure you he was already dead before we jumped in the water.

—He fucking wasn't. He was alive. He was fighting to get away from you, fighting for air, and you held him until he couldn't fight anymore.

—I didn't say he wasn't breathing. I said he was dead.

—What the fuck are you saying? I watch myself die and you come out with some clever shit. It was me down there. Me! *I* died.

—Then I rest my case. You, I assume, are still breathing and so was the boy. But he was dead, Lincoln, and so are you. I am not a murderer. I don't break down doors or force myself on people. I only go where I am wanted. I am always invited into a person's life, Lincoln, always. You were kind enough to create a space for me in yours and, hey presto, here I am!

Esurio spreads his arms wide as if he is introducing himself on a stage.

—I never invited you into my life.

—You never wrote a formal invitation, if that's what you mean, and if there had been someone to watch over you, then perhaps we might have been nothing more than casual acquaintances. But there was no one, Lincoln, no one.

I can't look at him, so I turn away and stare at the yellow diving board and the lifeless buildings in the distance. The surface of the water is calm now. It's as if the splash never happened, and I forget there is a dead boy at the bottom of the pool. When I turn back towards Esurio he is gone and I'm alone in this dead landscape. The chair and the building behind it look as if they have been there forever. Without any sign of life to disturb them, they seem indestructible and, without the chaos of splashing water, they are empty of meaning, neither dead nor alive. Just *there*. I long to stay in this place. Solid. Permanent. Calm.

I lift a tiny pebble off the patio and throw it into the water. It barely makes a ripple but one small splash brings everything back to life and paves the way for a bigger splash to follow. As I watch the small crack in the water begin to heal, like the closing of a wound, I think of the boy, of my life and countless other lives, opening the same wound over and over again, before disappearing without trace under the water, and I think of the many lives buried so deep in this great big sea of loneliness and fear that we forget they were lives worth saving.

The Day After the Bigger Splash

When I wake up, the sheets are soaking wet. I look at the wall behind the bed. It's white. I touch it and press it. It's cold and hard. I fall out of bed and in a few minutes I'm walking along Dean Street. The day passes. I am pissed by lunchtime and totally fucked by three in the afternoon.

8 p.m.

I meet Suzie at my flat. We fuck for a couple of hours and, long before I'm done, I'm thinking about the next line.

11 p.m.

I take Suzie into Soho House on Greek Street. In the reception area, a soap actor is standing chatting to a few friends. I am generally fucked off with actors. When I am hammered I want to kill them. He walks up to Suzie and asks:

—Do you know who I am?

She says she doesn't. He touches her arse and, when she struggles to pull away from him, I lunge at him and push him backwards over a chair. Two bouncers grab me from behind and throw me out onto Dean Street. I turn and go to headbutt the entrance to Soho House. Suzie shouts at me:

—No, Linc, please no.

I charge at the door and miss it. My head cracks against the wall. The blood gets in my eyes. Suzie tries to wipe it away but she can't get near me. I pass out making a second charge at the wall.

2 a.m.

I meet Maynard in Little Italy. I have a plaster on my head. I don't know how it got there.

We hang about the bar for a few minutes before he passes out. I leave him propped him up in a corner and look across to see Esurio lying in the floor, a glass of absinthe in one hand, staring up a Wrap's skirt. He smiles and pokes his tongue at me before sliding up through the Wrap's body. She shivers and looks around as he floats over to me:

—I am so pleased you are still with us. I'm sure you will die a thousand times before it's finally over, but you know the end is coming, Lincoln. Two trials in the New Year and then . . .

—I don't give a fuck about the trials. I don't give a fuck about my life. I don't give a fuck about anything.

—I know, and that's what makes you so beautiful and pathetic. *The Great Lincoln Townley: Dead and Unmourned.*

He passes me a tray covered in coke and I take it all.

December 2010. Six Things I Remember About Christmas

He doesn't bother with me as much as he used to. It's like he knows he doesn't have to try anymore. He's won and he's bored with his triumph:

—Don't expect a challenge and a reward like last Christmas. I'm afraid the rewards this year are all mine.

I black out for most of December. This is what I remember:

- I'm sitting in The Office and I notice my rate of indifference is off the scale. I don't want to die running anymore nor do I want to live. I don't care either way. I feel like I'm already dead. All I care about is the next line and the next drink.
- I think I fuck a lot of Wraps and a handful of Grannies in December but I can't be sure of numbers. I get no pleasure from doing it, only from talking about it afterwards. They call me *Mr Viagra* or *The Soho Shagger*. At least Glory makes the tedium of pounding tolerable.
- I'm telling a story to the boys in The Office when a guy on the next table laughs and says:
  —Hey, Casanova, answer this: if a tree falls in the forest and no one hears it, does it make a sound?
I knock him out with a punch to the side of the neck.
- I spend Christmas Day with my Mum. She says:
  —Lincoln, you look terrible and I'm really worried for you. I think it's impossible for anyone be really worried for me. Esurio says:
  —You're not worth a thought, Lincoln, never mind a second one. And I believe him.
- I turn thirty-nine just after Christmas. I get hammered as usual. I am almost the same age as my father when he died. I think about him for a moment. Then I forget.

- I'm walking down Frith Street when I see the boy at
  the bottom of the pool. He looks different. I look
  again. It's definitely me. I recognise the terror in his
  eyes and the boy is holding his hand out towards me
  as I get near him. I ignore him. When I look back,
  his face changes. I can't read the expression. Anger.
  Pain. I don't care. He's still a boy. He reaches out to
  me again. I ignore him a second time and carry on
  walking. I think:
  —What the fuck does he want from me?
  Then I think:
  —Whatever it is, I can't give it. We have nothing to
    say to each other. When I look back over my
    shoulder, he's gone.

New Year's Eve. 8 p.m.

The Townhouse on Dean Street is heaving. I ran out of coke
this morning. I haven't had a line all day and the craving is
intense. I reach into my pocket to get my phone. My dealer
will be around Soho. My pocket is empty. I check the other
side. Empty. I get up off the bar stool and check my trouser
pockets. Nothing. I forget about the phone and begin to panic.
I MUST have a line. I turn my jacket pockets inside out to see
if there are any grains of coke in there. I can't see any but I lick
them anyway just to be on the safe side. Terry sees me and
says:
   —What the fuck are you doing?
   I look at him:
   —Have you got any gear?

—No.

—Do you know anyone who has?

—No.

—Then fucking leave me alone, then.

I run back to my flat. Two Wraps are fucking each other in my bed. I ask them:

—Coke! Do you have any coke?

They look into my eyes and can't speak. They shake their heads and pull the duvet cover over their naked bodies, as I start turning the place inside out. I think:

—How the fuck can I not have any coke on New Year's Eve?

I empty every drawer and throw them all across the room. The last one hits the wall and breaks apart. I ask the Wraps.

—Who's your dealer?

They tell me and I say:

—Well fucking call him then.

One of them picks up her phone and makes the call.

—Sorry, Linc, it's ringing out.

I leave the flat and head towards the Dirty Dance Strip Club. There's a guy who bangs a lot of the Wraps who work there and I score off him sometimes. He'll be there. When I get there one of the floor managers comes up to me and says:

—Would you like a table sir?

—Do I look like I want a fucking table?

He says something into a phone. I pass from table to table, looking for the guy with the gear. He isn't in. Some Wraps hassle me. I tell them to fuck off. I look over to the stage and Esurio is curling himself around one of the poles. Behind him is a curtain. His voice cuts through the music, as he gestures to a fucking mountain of coke behind the curtain:

—Yours, Lincoln, all yours.

I run towards the stage. There are people blocking my way. I know them. My son, my Mum, my Dad, my whole fucking family, old friends, people who looked out for me as a kid, they're all there and I push them out of the way. One after another they fall like skittles. I don't care who they are. I don't care who I hurt. I MUST have some coke. MUST. MUST. MUST. There is nothing in common between me and the people who stand in my way, especially those who throw up a barrier and call it love. We are a different species. We do not share anything. We cannot communicate. Not now. Not ever.

The Day of Judgement

I am preparing for two Court Appearances in eight weeks. The first one is a week from now and the second one about a month after that. People around Soho, those who know about this shit, are being really nice to me. Maynard says:

—You'll be all right, Linc. Think of the court as a stage and you'll even enjoy it.

Some of my Regulars send me texts. Here's a few:

U r a star! Luv u. Suzie x

Blow job when you win! XXXX S.

Talk as good as you bang and you'll win easy! X Jen

Fuck them like u fuck me. Slurps. Simone.

I get about thirty. Most of them include pictures as an added incentive. I show them to the boys in The Office. They are used to seeing my messages from Wraps. I hate their indifference, so I show them the picture message from Katie. She has a butt plug in her arse:

One for me and one for the judge! Kisses. K

They like that and I feel proud of myself.

Meeting My Barrister

Two days before my First Court Appearance, Benjamin, my lawyer, who handles most of the cases for the *Lost Men of Soho*, introduces me to my barrister, Tristram. I think:

How can a man called Tristram defend me?

I know Benjamin, who looks as if he might be as comfortable in the dock as out of it, is thinking the same. As the meeting kicks off, he nods at me as if to say:

—You're fucking lucky to get anyone to defend you, so please be polite to Tristram.

I am. Very polite. Things are going well in the opening exchanges until he ruins it:

—I think you should plead guilty to the charge.

—But it's assaulting a police officer. I could serve time for that.

—While that's true I can only advise you professionally and we can put up some strong mitigation.

—What mitigation?

—Well, you were provoked in the bar at Ronnie Scott's, followed into the toilets, and, by the time the police arrived, you were beside yourself with confusion. I also understand you had your penis out at the time because you had been urinating and you had not had time to adjust yourself. You, therefore, faced a very humiliating situation.

—Is that it?

—That's the best we can do, I'm afraid.

—But there were no witnesses and I have my side to the story.

—I'm sure you do have your side of the story, and I will do my best to convey it to the judge. However, there was a witness and it is not good for you.

—What fucking witness?

Benjamin gives me a look.

—Sorry, what witness?

—CCTV. It was all caught on camera. The police officer is merely trying to restrain you when you engage in a flurry of headbutts, punches and kicks. Given the strength of this evidence, it will work in your favour to plead guilty and to be contrite.

When I get back to The Office, Simon asks:

—How did you get on?

—I've got to plead guilty and be contrite.

—That's not like you, Linc. What does it mean?

—It means I'm fucked.

My First Court Appearance

I sit in a dock flanked by two police officers. We all stand when the judge comes in. He looks over at me. I catch an impression of contempt. I smile. Not too creepily. Just a little show of respect. It doesn't work. He gives me the same look again, only this time it's laced with a sneer.

Tristram puts up as good a show as he can. A couple of Regulars and one Occasional are sitting in the public gallery. I smile at them. One of them rolls her tongue at me. The judge sees her doing it. I wish she hadn't done it. The day whizzes by in a flurry of legal argument. After about an hour I have a thought:

—This is great. It'll soon be over and I can get hammered in The Office.

This thought recurs throughout the day, growing in

strength during the afternoon. The stronger it gets, the more untouchable I feel. I think:

—And after I get hammered I'll celebrate by banging the two Regulars and the Occasional in my flat.

In a recess, while we wait for the judge to consider the verdict, Tristram calls me into a small meeting room.

—Have you brought an overnight bag?

—What for? If he can't sort himself out and pass a sentence by close of play what's he want me to do? Sleep in the dock?

—No, of course not.

His tone reminds me I'm a bit of leftover dinner on his shoe. He finishes:

—You may face a short custodial sentence and, if that is the case, you will be taken to prison directly from the court.

I feel the blood drain from my face and hands. The same thought goes round and round my head:

No drink. No coke. No cunt. And no Telling in The Office.

I'm still in shock when we are called back into the court. The judge rattles on for what seems like forever. I don't hear a word of it until:

—... and I therefore sentence you, Mr Townley, to pay a fine of one thousand two hundred pounds plus costs, and to attend an anger management course, the details of which will be specified by your Probation Officer.

I am ecstatic as I make my way out of the court. I get into a taxi with the Wraps. One of them wanks me off on the way to Soho. The boys have champagne on ice and applaud when I walk into The Office.

My Second Court Appearance

In the days after being released by the court, my mood returns to the black indifference that has become so familiar to me now. The Anger Management course makes me angry. I want to punch the tutor, a smug-looking, professor type, who tries to be 'one of us' by wearing jeans and a T-shirt. He speaks with the kind of well-meaning *earnestness* which is stained with dishonesty. I'd rather be taught by a cold-blooded killer. At least he'd make me feel human. I make a point of turning up every day in a jacket, my trademark handkerchief popping out of the top pocket. I don't punch the tutor but, after the fourth session, I get into an argument with another of the losers on the course when he pushes me in the back and the tea I'm carrying spills on my shirt. I turn and, as I hit him, I just catch him saying:

—Sorry, it was an acc—

No one saw us and he is still conscious, so I pick him up and apologise:

—Sorry, man. Keep this between us, yeah?

He nods. He wants to kill me but I am stronger than him. So he nods.

Meeting My Barrister – Again

I have the same barrister for my Second Court Appearance. It feels like *Groundhog Day*:

—I'm afraid I recommend you go guilty this time too. There is some CCTV evidence of you beating up the paparazzi, as well as several witness statements including three from officers involved in your arrest and, as for possession of cocaine, the substance was in your pocket with your finger-prints on the paper.

—I suppose I'd better take an overnight bag this time too?

—Best to be on the safe side, although there is much stronger mitigation this time.

—Like what?

—You were struck first by one of the paparazzi and you were clearly concerned for the safety of the women in your company. You were then set upon by four paparazzi, who retreated when they realised they were no match for you physically. Your only crime is to exact such ferocious retribution you could easily have killed one or more of them. The fact that you ripped your shirt off only strengthens the prosecution case that, rather than walk away to safety, you wanted to satisfy your desire for revenge at any cost.

—What are the chances of me being sent down?

—Thirty per cent.

—So it's in my favour.

—Statistically, yes.

—What other measure is there other than numbers?

He looks at me without answering.

My Second Court Appearance

In the week before the case I receive over seventy texts from Wraps and mates. Most are the same as the last ones but I get a special one from a Hungarian Occasional called Natasha:

You stood for me. I remember. Good luck! Natasha.

It was in Nobu in Mayfair. We were in the bar downstairs

going through the menu when a guy started hassling her. I told him to back off. He didn't listen so I stood up, grabbed him by the wrist, and began squeezing. He felt my rage coursing through his veins. I said:

—Back off or I'll snap your wrist and, if you're not out of this restaurant in one minute, I'll break your neck.

He made the mistake of looking into my eyes when I said it. I could feel the fear in his wrist. He went out so fast it looked like a sprint to the door. When he was gone, Natasha kissed me on the cheek.

—No one protect me before. No one. Thanking you.

I banged her that night and we still do it about once every couple of months.

When I walk into court, there are six Regulars in the public gallery. They smile but I can see they're frightened. I care less for myself than they do. I do not understand their love.

The trial lasts two days. Most of the time is spent on technical arguments. All I want to do is drink and snort and fuck. During his summing-up, the judge says:

—Your behaviour, Mr Townley, was lamentable. You are clearly a violent man with little or no control over your actions. You attacked those men with no concern whatsoever over their safety. In fact, I believe your motives were more sinister than simple lack of concern. It is my conviction based on the evidence that you wanted to hurt those photographers.

I look across at Tristram. He gives no indication of what he's feeling. The longer the judge goes on, the worse I feel. By the time he reaches the end, I'm preparing myself for ten years inside. I want to say:

—I care less about my fate than you. Do your worst. I am beyond pain.

Somehow I restrain myself. I'm glad about that. The punishment is a fine. I'm out. Back in The Office, I'm getting hammered with Maynard, Terry, Steve, Simon and a brothelload of Wraps. By about midnight I'm as fucked as I've ever been. Esurio is keeping a track of everything I'm taking. At one point he is jumping with excitement and he says:

—I feel the end is near, Lincoln. No one can take this much alcohol and cocaine and wake up anything other than delirious beyond measure. To be acquitted by a stranger and then executed by your own hand, and all on the same day! Poetic justice, Lincoln, poetic justice!

At some point I pass out and, when I wake up, The Office is shut and I am alone, slumped on a table near the back. There's a small fridge behind the bar where Mario always puts my unfinished bottles. I'm shaking and my heart is pounding. The sweat is pouring down my face and a tsunami of anxiety floods every cell of my nervous system. I need a drink. I stagger over to the fridge and pull out a bottle of red wine. It is almost full and I take it back to the table. I begin drinking from the bottle but I can't stop shaking and the wine splashes over my face and jacket. I grab the neck of the bottle with two hands to steady myself but that seems to make it worse. By the time the bottle is empty, half of it is on my face and clothes. I collapse onto the table. I try to make out what time it is. I can't see the hands on my watch. I move my wrist back and forth to help me focus. I think it's ten past five in the morning. Mario will be here in just over an hour. I need a piss. I can't move and a warm liquid flows down my leg. I can't think straight. My brain is mush. Strange noises howl in my head. Dark shadows dance around me. My world is twisting and melting and I know I'm dying. I open my eyes for what I'm sure will be the last time. I see Esurio behind the bar, sitting on a large, throne-like chair. He pours himself some drinks and lays out a number of lines. He snorts a few, waves his handkerchief across his nose and sniffs in my direction before he finishes a glass of absinthe and bangs his cane on the floor.

—Lincoln Maximilian Townley, I accuse you of the crime of Treachery. Stand up at the table as I speak to you and the first witness will come into the courtroom.

I am strangely sober and able to stand. I turn to see who he is and I watch him as he walks towards me. He is perhaps a little shorter than me and wearing a suit and tie. I am sure I recognise his walk and the way his body moves. I pick up a familiar smell of tobacco drifting towards me. When he gets close enough our eyes meet and when I realise who he is, my legs give way under me and I grip the table to stop myself from falling.

—How? How can it be you?

The short dark hair, parted at the side, the broad reassuring shoulders, the smile I haven't seen in decades. He stops maybe ten feet away from me and looks at me. I hold his gaze and we stay like that until Esurio breaks the silence and addresses my accuser:

—Lincoln John Townley, you are the father of the accused, Lincoln Maximilian Townley?

—Yes I am.

—You wish to bring a charge against your son of Treachery.

—I do.

—You are certain of the charge and you are ready to produce evidence of his Treachery?

—I am.

—And who has the accused betrayed?

—Himself.

—Lincoln Maximilian Townley, you have heard from your accuser. How do you plead?

I'm gasping for air and my legs feel so light I think they're going to buckle under me. My voice is slow and croaky:

—I don't understand ... How can I be charged with ... Treachery against myself?

—Lincoln, please enter a plea.

I can barely speak.

—Not ... guilty ...

—Please proceed with the cross-examination.

For a long while Dad doesn't speak. We are both sponges, absorbing each other, measuring the changes since we last met, one small fragment at a time. His face is sad and warm until he looks down at the ground, takes a deeper breath, and, when he looks up, his expression has changed. It is stronger now, more determined, ready to say what he has come to say.

—I'm sorry to be the one who has to do this.

—But how? How have I betrayed myself?

—More ways than I can remember. I wanted everything for you. I wanted you to grow up strong and be someone your Mum could be proud of, to be there for her and make something of yourself. You're smart, a better salesman than I ever was, perhaps one of the best, and you could have done better for yourself. How much money have you earned?

—I don't know. Loads over the years.

—And how much have you got left?

—Nothing.

—Do you own a house?

—No.

—A car?

—No.

—So what have you done with all your talent? Where have you wasted it?

I lower my head. Esurio intervenes:

—Please display the first exhibit.

A screen drops down behind the bar and a film begins to play. It shows me around Soho drinking, snorting, fighting. It lasts a few minutes but the scenes move so fast it feels like my life in Soho played out in seconds. I see all the people I know, The Boss and the staff at The Club, the boys at The Office and countless Wraps, as I have never seen them before. When my back is turned, sometimes they carry on laughing or just ignore me, but often they share a look. I have never seen this look before. They look at me with *concern*. I see them caring for me, maybe for just a moment, before I beat the concern out of them with another act of heroic stupidity. I cannot imagine I am worth anything at all except a moment's entertainment, a funny obituary and a wake Caligula would be proud of. But that look is real and I never saw it until now.

The film ends and my father continues:

—You stamp all over what other people give you. They care for you and you waste their love.

Dad looks up at Esurio who says:

—Play the second exhibit.

It's a few weeks after Dad died, and Mum is in the kitchen of our council house. She is sat at the kitchen table alone. I think she is crying. Then I see her as she is now, maybe a little older, putting flowers on a grave. I think they are for Dad but they are for me. The stone reads:

Lincoln Maximilian Townley
1972 − 2012
Aged 40 years

No fancy words. Just a name and some numbers. I wonder how I died. Dad looks at me:

—You let us all down, Lincoln. You betrayed me, your Mum, all of us. Above all, you betrayed yourself. This isn't the life I wanted for you and it's not what I want for you now. I'm here because I want you to live a longer life than me.

These words cut into me like a knife. They are an assault on my heart and I snap with rage:

—Care? Because you care? It's too fucking late for that now. *You* left *me*. Remember? In a fucking caravan park. I was a kid and you just dropped down and left.

—I couldn't help that.

—Yes you could. You could have smoked less, you could have looked after yourself better, you could have lived like I was worth sticking around for. But you didn't. At least I'm a fighter. If I get knocked down, I get back up again. I don't quit. Never. Not like you. You quit on me and all of us. You show me a film of Mum crying. What for? *You* should have been there with her. Not me. You. That was your job as a husband and a father. To be there for us. But you quit. And yeah I messed up my life. I drink too much, fight too much, fuck too much. But you should be standing where I am and I should be the one accusing you and you know what the charge is? Neglect. I loved you. I looked up to you. I wanted to be like you and then you fucked off. Two of us died in that caravan park. You died and there was a body and a funeral. But I died too. I died on the inside and no one gave a fuck.

They didn't even know. And now, after all these years, you come back here and accuse me of Treachery. I am not guilty, you hear me, not guilty.

—Maybe you're right. Maybe I didn't live my life well enough and it was taken off me. I've spent years watching you get angry and fight and run and I need to know that I died for *something*.

—So it's all about you?

—No ...

—What's it about then?

—It's about you, son. I want to know that I didn't wreck your life when I lost mine.

I stare at him. I want to take him in. Cut the distance between us. He goes on:

—And it's about Lewis.

Esurio bangs his cane on the ground:

—Play the third exhibit.

A film begins. It's about nine o'clock yesterday and Lewis is sitting next to me in The Office as I celebrate winning my court case. I am hammered. He is trying to talk to me:

—Dad, I'm worried about you. About us.

I hug him and laugh.

—Fucking hell, Lewis, we're fine. I love you, son, you know that.

—I know, Dad, but you're not hearing me.

A Wrap comes and sits on my lap. He ignores her.

—Dad, I'm losing you. We're losing each other. I'm going to lose you just like you lost your Dad.

—Don't be stupid. I'm fucking invincible.

He grabs me by the lapel. I use every ounce of restraint to

stop myself from decking him.

—You're not, Dad. You're killing yourself. You scare me. I love you.

He gets up and leaves. I can't make out what I say as he walks away.

The film stops.

I look at Esurio.

—Did that happen last night? Is it real?

He laughs at me.

—Is anything in your life real, Lincoln?

I look him in the eye:

—I change my plea. I am guilty as charged. Guilty!

He smiles. It's like he has squeezed everything out of me and there is nothing left for him to do except to pass sentence:

—Lincoln Maximilian Townley, you have finally been held to account for your crimes. Yours is a dissolute life devoted only to your own pleasure with complete disregard for the feelings of others. While I do not doubt your good nature, it is a nature you have buried so deep you may never be able to retrieve it. Your father was a decent man who did his best to guide you but you betrayed him, you betrayed his memory and you betrayed yourself. You have also betrayed the love you have for your son and the love he has for you. For such flagrant abuse of the man you could have been, the court has only one sentence it is able to pass: Death. I will now remove the defendant from the court and take him to a place where the sentence can be carried out immediately.

Esurio leaps over the bar and seems to float over to me. He is leering. Triumphant.

—This, Lincoln, is where our magnificent friendship was always going to end. May I thank for so many unforgettable nights. You have been a tremendous sport.

He grabs me by my arms, pulls me out from behind the table and drags me along the floor. I am shocked at his strength. I am a baby in his hands. I have never been in the grip of such power. I don't even struggle. I know there is no escape.

He throws me out of The Office onto the street. I gasp for air and my limbs flail about as I look to steady myself. When I get to my feet, I can't see Esurio anywhere. I let out an enormous scream and collapse to my knees.

So-Ho!

Dawn. I can still hear my scream echoing through the streets. My body is lying flat on the ground. When I open my eyes, I can make out a strip club, a theatre and a casino. I check for feeling in my limbs. Everything feels fine. I run my hands across my face and head. There is no blood. The same words bounce around my head like bullets:

—You scare me. I love you. You scare me. I love you.

Soho is my personal asylum and I stand and wait for Esurio to bring me my straightjacket for the last time. He is coming. I sense him. I look around and I notice there are no people on the street. There are lights everywhere and I can even smell food and spices but no one eats, no one drinks. I look behind me into The Office. It's empty too. There are glasses, cutlery and plates on the tables, but there is not a person in sight. I am in a concrete desert.

Then I hear Esurio's voice, shrill and thick, letting out a hunting call that hasn't been heard on these streets for centuries:

—SO-HO! SO-HO! SO-HO!

The call echoes through Soho like a roar and it's followed by the sound of a hunting horn. In the distance I hear the sound of hooves. Running. Towards me. I look to my right and I see Esurio on the back of a horse, dressed in what looks like full hunting gear, blowing a large, ornate hunting horn. He is being followed by packs of hounds, big and wild, like the beast that cornered me in the Charing Cross Hotel. As soon as he sees me, he begins to gallop and the hounds follow, pounding towards me. I run, turn into Dean Street then left into Richmond Buildings, and burst through the main entrance of the Soho Hotel. Like everywhere else in Soho, it is lifeless but the tables in the ground floor bar area are laid for dinner as usual. I jump over them, sending cutlery and plates crashing to the floor. I hear the hounds barking in the lobby and I sprint out onto Wardour Street, barring the back entrance of the hotel with a piece of scaffolding. I look behind me and see them salivating at the door, their exit blocked as they see me run onto Broadwick Street.

I pause for a moment to catch my breath. Above the sound of the horn and the barking of the hounds, I can hear the same words:

—You scare me. I love you. You scare me. I love you.

I am running for my life without fear and I know with absolute certainty that I want to live. I WANT TO LIVE. Perhaps the feeling has come too late but at least I have felt it and touched it, and when the hounds rip me to pieces they will take my life but they can't kill this feeling. It's the one thing Esurio can't take.

I look down towards the market stalls and see them tumbling as the hounds tear through them. I run onto Broadwick Street. In a few strides I'm at the junction of Poland Street and the pack is closing on me. I turn to run up towards Oxford Street but then I see hounds and Esurio charging down Poland Street towards me. I turn down Lexington Street and, by the time I reach Brewer Street, I can almost feel the breath of the pack on my back. Above the howl of the hounds, I hear him, delirious, anticipating the kill:

—SO-HO! SO-HO! SO-HO!

I am moments from Death. I can taste it. If it has to be over, I want it to be over. Quickly. The thought of my flesh being stripped off my bones drives me to the edge of madness. I keep running. Running like I always have, pain snapping at my heels, driving me on to the next drink, the next line, the next Wrap.

I stop.

I am tired of running.

Let them take me.

I am outside a sex shop on Brewer Street when I turn to face them:

—Come on! Come on! Let's fucking do it!

Esurio rides up to the door of the sex shop and dismounts. He raises his hand and the hounds stop. He moves towards me and the hounds move with him. I back onto the pavement. The neon lights of the sex shop are flickering behind me. Slowly I step backwards into the shop and I'm surrounded by magazines, DVDs, vibrators, dildos and S&M gear. Esurio follows me in. I shout at him:

—Hardly a fair fight is it?

—Fairness, Lincoln, has nothing to do with it. The time has come. It is over.

Some of the lights inside the shop have failed, but even though it's dark I can see him pull a pack of porn playing cards off a shelf near the door. He opens the pack and takes four cards from the top:

—Look closely at the cards, Lincoln . . .

I look once. Twice. A third time just to make sure. The first card shows me banging a Wrap in the disabled toilets at The Office; another shows me decking a copper in Ronnie Scott's, while a third shows me running alone down Wardour Street in the early hours of the morning, clenching my teeth and pressing my hand against the pain in my chest.

—. . . and you will see your entire life: you conquer, you fight and all the while you are dying of loneliness . . .

He turns the fourth card over. It shows my body, torn to pieces, on the floor where we are standing.

—. . . and I'm left to claim what you owe me. Your life. Your soul. You are mine. You have always been mine. You belong to me.

—Not any more. I've had enough.

Facing death, I have never felt more alive. *You scare me. I love you.* These six words stretch like a bridge between what I was and the man I want to be. I know the bridge is real, connecting one life to another and, what passes across it, sustains me. I give it a name. I call it Hope.

Esurio sneers at me:

—Enough? You don't know the meaning of the word. You never have and you never will. Before you die, take one last moment of madness, Lincoln. In memory of the King of Soho.

He waves his gloved hand like a magician. Mountains of cocaine and endless bottles of wine, beer and champagne stretch out behind him, as more naked Wraps than I have ever seen in one place, fuck each other.

—All this, Lincoln, is yours. Take it now.

I look at the seething mass of bodies. I feel a slight twist in my gut and my cock flickers, like it's about to burn, then it dissolves into nothing.

—I don't want it. It means nothing to me anymore.

I can hear the hounds growling outside on Brewer Street. Esurio looks puzzled.

—Come to me, Lincoln, come to me.

—No.

—Come to me, now!

I look into his eyes. They are frantic and I see for the first time how much he *needs* me. He needs me with a hunger I have never seen before. He *can't* kill me. The hounds *can't* attack. All they can do is wait for me to walk into their jaws. And if I refuse to walk . . .

—No, I won't come to you again, not now, not ever.

—Please, Lincoln, we belong together, you and I. Think of all the great times we've had, the places we've been. The Office, Bungalow 8, Ronnie Scott's, Little Italy, The Box, Grouchos, the Sanderson, Jet Black, we even went to the Cannes Film Festival together. Does that count for nothing?

—It did once. It doesn't anymore.

—Well, ask yourself this. How many ladies would you have seduced without me? How many fights would you have won? Who bestowed upon you the title *The King of Soho*? It was me, Lincoln, me. I have been with you longer than you know. I have been there for you all your life and, just when we reach the peak of our relationship, you abandon me. Just look at everything that surrounds me and remember the pleasure, Lincoln, remember it, feel it in every cell of your body . . .

I look at the coke and the booze and the Wraps. I see some naked Grannies begging me to pound them.

—. . . and never let it go, Lincoln, never. Think what you

will lose. A life of denial is not a life for you. I will call the hounds off. I will overturn the verdict of the court. You can have all this and live, Lincoln, live like you always dreamed of living.

I wipe my hand across my mouth. I look at Esurio. He angles his body to the side and I take a step towards the booze and the gear. The twisting in my stomach gets more intense. I see a Wrap going down on a Granny. I want them. I want everything and more, much more. Esurio smiles:

—You see, it's in you. You can't deny it. Feed me, Lincoln, feed me.

I close my eyes and see a wooden bridge, suspended over a deep valley. As I cross the bridge, I see Esurio cutting the ropes that keep the bridge from falling into the valley. I know if I let him cut the ropes, nothing will ever cross that bridge again. I rush towards him and when he knows he hasn't got enough time to cut the rope, he tries to run but I grab him by the arm and, in the struggle to break free, he slips and I watch his body spin and fall but the valley is too deep and I don't see it hit the ground. As he falls, I stand on the bridge shouting:

—Enough ... Enough ... Enough ...

I open my eyes and the Wraps, the coke, the booze and the Grannies are gone. Esurio is gone too. There are punters in the shop and a man holding a gag and an S&M DVD is looking at me:

—Are you OK, mate? You've been standing there just staring at the door for ages.

—Yeah. I'm fine, thanks.

When I walk out onto Brewer Street, the hounds have disappeared. There are people around. Laughing, talking, living. I see a red stiletto lying on the pavement and it looks lost and alone. I pick it up and, as I touch it I think how beautiful it is and I think of all the beauty in these streets, the kind of beauty that brings people from all the cities and countries of the world to worship here, and I know if there is a God, he is the God of these pilgrims who travel across continents to find each other in a magical place I am seeing for the first time: Soho.

CORK CITY LIBRARIES

Epilogue

May 2011

I'm looking for Lincoln John Townley.

—When did he die?

—Nineteen eighty-six.

—Give me a minute.

A woman in her late thirties gets out a plan of the cemetery and rolls it out on the table. I notice her nail varnish matches the red flowers on her summer dress and the bouquet of roses I have in my hand. She is efficient, kind and ordinary. From the ring on her finger I see she is married and I guess she has a couple of kids at home. I map out her life in my head. Marriage. Kids. Work. Retirement. Death. Interspersed with the odd dinner party, the guilt of a misplaced kiss, holidays abroad and mild depression. I am jealous of her. The invisible ordinariness of it all. She gives me directions to my father's grave. I thank her and leave.

It's been nearly three months since I had a drink or took a line. Occasionally I think about it but it passes. Although I attend occasional AA meetings, I do not follow the Steps. I go to see what I don't want to be and to measure the reassuring distance between the suffering of others and my own situation. After the last meeting I made a list of things I have noticed about myself since my last drink:

- I am exercising just as much, possibly more
- When I'm running, I able to look around me and see there is a world beyond the end of my breath
- I often visit the Tate Modern and the National Portrait Gallery. I pick maybe half a dozen paintings and give myself time to sit with them
- I still bang Wraps, although they are much fewer in number and I have lost interest in turning a fuck into a media event
- I don't even call them Wraps anymore. They are women
- I think I'm capable of loving a woman for the first time
- I hardly ever think about Esurio. I thought I would miss him but I don't
- There are times, more than I ever thought possible, when I think I'm actually worth something
- I am a father and a son
- I no longer feel less than my son. I *know* that my son is more than me
- I am grateful I am alive
- I sometimes feel sorry for the things I did but most of the time I don't
- Generally I feel good, but occasionally something bothers me. I struggle to describe it in words. I can't even name it. One night I had this dream:

I am sick. Usually I shake off an infection but this time it goes on for days and gets worse. Eventually I go to see the doctor and he gives me a small bottle of medicine. I tell him I'm very ill and he reassures me I will be well soon. I get up to leave the surgery but when I reach the door I stop, look at the small bottle of medicine and ask: Are you sure this is enough? Are you sure?

I woke up sweating, my heart beating and, when I tried to get back to sleep, the words kept bouncing around my head: *Are you sure this is enough? Are you sure?*

I place the roses down on the grave and feel inside my jacket pocket. I pull out the silver key I've kept in my bedside table. As I bury it by the headstone, I think:

—I never found which door it opens.

I am about to leave when I feel a fly land on my neck. I swat it away. Another lands, and another, until there must be a dozen of them, buzzing around my head. I hear a familiar voice:

—I never thought I would see you here.

I turn and see a man standing by a tree. He is perhaps twenty feet away but the stench he gives off makes me feel sick. He looks like he has just been released from a concentration camp. His skin is covered in sores and wrapped so tight around his bones I'm sure it's about to tear like paper. He is balancing on a walking stick that looks like it might once have been quite fashionable but is now so worn that all the varnish has come off and the wood is rotting. The long, black coat he's wearing has almost completely disintegrated, as have his shirt and trousers. His feet are bare and, as I look closer, I notice his skin and clothes seem to be moving. I take a step towards him and gasp as I see his entire body is crawling with insects. The flies that disturbed me are living on him. There are other insects, too: caterpillars, spiders, cockroaches. His face breaks into a half-smile and it's then that I recognise him.

—Esurio?

There's a long pause while he just stares at me.

—Ah, so you know who I am, even when you see me like this. Bravo, Lincoln, bravo.

His voice is frail and barely rises above a whisper.

—What happened to you?

—Nothing happened to me.

—But you're so old and ... dying ...

—You think I have ever looked any different?

—Of course you have. You used to be so fashionable and handsome. And that was only a few months ago.

—No. You are wrong. I have always been as you see me now. The well-dressed man you knew was just the man you chose to see. If you had eyes then as you do now, this is what you would have seen. Look at me. Could you believe in a man like this? Could you follow him, Lincoln? It's a source of great sadness to me that I can no longer hide myself from you.

We stand facing each other for what seems like forever until I tell him:

—I have to go now and I will never see you again.

His face hardens into irritation:

—You can't say that, Lincoln. Despite the way I look I will not die and I will never be far away from you. I agree there will be days when you will not think of me but there will be other days, many of your days, when you will pine for me like a lover, and there will be a Special Day we both know will come when you need me again and I promise I will be strong and dress well for the party. Until then, I want you to know, I am waiting, Lincoln, waiting, and my patience is ...

I don't hear the end of the sentence because I walk away from him, but when I reach the gates of the cemetery I look back. The strain of standing has taken its toll on him and he is leaning against the tree. Somehow his voice carries across the distance that separates us:

— ... endless, Lincoln, my patience is endless.

Afterword

There are people who knew me during my Soho years who cannot believe I am still alive. Neither can I.

When I think about those years, they are shocking, even to me.

I wanted to tell the story of my addiction to prove to myself I survived and to understand how I almost didn't. I wanted it to be fearless in its honesty, regardless of how I might be judged. It is based on real events and is, therefore, as politically incorrect and delusional as reality always is when looked at through honest eyes.

The story, of course, is not over. Although I have been dry for more than two years, I battle my addiction every day and I will do so for the rest of my life. In those two years I have not been in any fights nor have I been abusive to anyone. Well, hardly anyone. In the book my Mum says I'm a good lad and, when I'm sober, I like to think I am. She has stuck by me when I didn't deserve it and I will always love her and be there for her. Thanks to my brother Duncan for not judging me for what I have done. He's a good man whose even temper has often acted as a steadying influence in my life.

As the book shows, my dad, Lincoln, and my son, Lewis, were a big part of my recovery. They gave me a reason to want to stop the madness and I love them both more than words can say. However, the person who enabled me to see this, and without whom I would have never stopped drinking and using, is Dr Peter Hughes. He is a remarkable man who has helped many people clean up and find a way out of the prison of self-destruction and despair.

A heartfelt thank you to Denise for being in my life and to your amazing sons, Matthew and Louis, for allowing me into theirs.

I would especially like to thank James for being such a great and loving friend.

I no longer see most of the people I knew in my Soho years. I want them to know that this is not anything personal. It is a decision I have made as part of my recovery. Many will not understand my decision and will condemn me for writing this book. There is nothing I can do about that. What I can do is thank them for the good times and the bad.

I owe a huge debt of gratitude to my agent Carrie Kania and my editor Kerri Sharp for believing in the book.

Carrie asked me what advice I would give to an addict. I told her I don't feel equipped to advise anyone but, if I had to, I would say the first step is to admit you've got a problem and to reach out to anyone who can help. This can be your family, a friend, a professional addiction therapist or groups like Alcoholics Anonymous. While I didn't go the strict AA route, I do go to meetings occasionally and I provide support for other alcoholics as best as I am able. Above all, know that even in your darkest moments there is hope.

I want to end with a word about Esurio. He is, of course, fictional, although we have all met him at least once. Please take a moment now and remember your meeting with Esurio. It might make you more compassionate in the judgements you make about me because one day you might meet him again. As I say at the end of the book: Esurio is very patient and as keen to get to know you as he was to get to know me.